D0880849

SINGING FOR POWER

SINGING FOR POWER

The Song Magic of the Papago Indians
of Southern Arizona

Ruth Murray Underhill

University of California Press
Berkeley : 1938

UNIVERSITY OF CALIFORNIA PRESS
BERKELEY, CALIFORNIA

CAMBRIDGE UNIVERSITY PRESS
LONDON, ENGLAND

PRINTED IN THE UNITED STATES OF AMERICA
BY SAMUEL T. FARQUHAR, UNIVERSITY PRINTER

PREFACE

THE SONGS presented in the following pages form part of a longer study on Papago Ceremonies, which was made under the direction of the Humanities Council of Columbia University. The work occupied fourteen months spent in the Papago country, from June to October, 1931, and from February to October, 1933, and several shorter visits. It is impossible to name all my informants and interpreters, who numbered some forty-two, but I do heartily give them my warmest thanks. The songs were written down, first in the transmuted "song language," then in spoken Papago, then in literal translation, and finally in as accurate a free rendering as the structure of English would permit.

The illustrations which appear in the book are made from sketches drawn on the spot or from descriptions given by old Papago men and women. They are the work of two Indian boys, Avellino Herera and Sia Pueblo, and of another, Ben Pavisook, a Ute. I gladly acknowledge my indebtedness to them.

I would also express my gratitude to the two universities which have taken an interest in the work: to Columbia, which financed and directed it, and to California, which made its publication possible.

RUTH MURRAY UNDERHILL

Albuquerque, New Mexico
    July 1, 1937

CONTENTS

ELDER BROTHER'S PEOPLE

IN A DESERT CORNER of Arizona, where the Mexican boundary runs through valleys of sagebrush and mountains of sharp lava rock, lives a tribe of Indians who have never fought with the Whites. As a consequence, they are a people whom the Whites hardly know. The wolfish, feathered warrior who represents the Indian in popular art has become as standardized as the eagle on the coin, whereas the nonfighters have remained almost unknown. These peaceful Indians, who had something to live for when war was abolished, on their remote mesas and in their desert valleys still carry on, beneath their modern externals, a life based on other ideals than ours and aimed toward other goals.

Of such are the Papagos—Bean People, their neighbors called them. In the short, torrid, desert summer they sometimes could grow no other crop but their native beans, schooled to the heat and drought as is no other crop in the United States. In their language, the words that mean Bean People are a long series of sliding, whispered syllables; the Spaniards shortened them to Papago.

They were Spanish subjects once, when the ancient province of Pimería stretched from the mountains of Mexico up into a savage desert which is now called Arizona. They were the northernmost of all the Mexican tribes which spoke a language akin to the Aztec and they still use, in rude, brief form, the words of old Aztec prayers. They have games and ceremonies which echo those of extinct peoples, vanquished by the Spaniards on their northern march. Now that those once powerful neighbors are gone, we find in the manner of life of these blue-overalled cowboys of Arizona more of Mexican ceremony than remains in Mexico itself.

The Papagos are a gentle, poetic branch of the race which produced the Aztec conquerors. Squat, broad-faced, dark, often with the beauty of a clean-featured piece of sculpture, they have three chief characteristics. They never raise their voices; even the lustiest men speak in a smiling undertone which causes white traders to declare that these Indians must all know lip reading. Their movements are deliberate; our own swift jerkiness can hardly comprehend the rhythm slowed down by desert heat to the slow swing of a wave under a ship's bow in a dead calm. And they are always laughing. We who pass days, even weeks, at hard work, with no more than a polite smile now and then, can scarcely accustom ourselves to the gentle laughter which always accompanies Papago talk. No group of Papago men or women is ever together without the sound of it. Going back to New York after months of that sound, I have missed it as I would miss cold water if I could never drink it again.

That same laughter and those same slow movements have been going on in the same desert since prehistoric time. Other Indians have migrated here and there, but the Bean People were found by the first Spaniards just where they are now. They were found, and they were left again. The conquistadores, pushing through flood and forest up from Mexico City, found this barren northern country too much for even them to handle. The missionaries came and, at last, went. Even the Americans, stampeding westward after gold, steered clear of the rainless desert.

So the Papagos wandered, calm and smiling, back and forth across the waste of brilliant barrenness which Elder Brother, their god, had given them. They shot the ground squirrels and the rats and birds. They picked the caterpillars from the bushes. They shook the seeds from every blade of wild grass. They brushed the spines from cactus stems and roasted them for hours in a pit with a fire over it.

The native heath of the Desert People

I have never heard one of them object to this plan of life. Rather, an old woman telling me of it sighed and said: "To you Whites, Elder Brother gave wheat and peaches and grapes. To us, he gave the wild seeds and the cactus. Those are the *good* foods."

Of course, there was the deer. Elder Brother made him by slitting a desert mouse up the middle and giving it a deer heart. Then he put the deer on the hills with directions that, "when its time had come," it should offer itself to the hunter to be killed. But its time did not come any too often. Neither did the heat and the cloudbursts of the desert summer allow the beans and corn and squash to be more than an occasional blessing.

In winter there was no water, even to drink, except in the springs in the mountains. Each family sought one and lived there under the open sky finding what food it could until May, "the painful moon," when there was almost nothing left. Then, miraculously, unwatered, the desert began to bud. The clouds gathered and at last, in July, the rains fell.

> In all directions [says the Papago song]
> There is soft thunder.

Back came the people from the mountains to hold ceremonies that would "pull down the clouds." Suddenly came the moon of rain, and

> Although the ditches seemed deep enough
> And needing no more digging,
> Full to the brim they were,
> With rubbish piled high at the edges.

The desert, from a dry floor glaring like slag under the heat, became a stately garden of green shrubs and tropical flowers. Then it was time for every man to drop his digging stick into the earth and let fall four corn kernels in the hole, and for his wife, following behind him, to push the earth over them with her bare foot. The little hard corn, in ears six inches long, came up "like a feather headdress," and the squash and beans came up "singing together." For two months the desert possessed its summer beauty. Then the rain ceased falling, the water holes began to shrink, the moon of dry grass came, and the desert was desert again. Sometimes the rains came too late and there was no corn. "Then we dug roots and sifted grass seeds all summer."

It was a life so stern that the chief need was not for food but for mere drinking water. It was hardly worth while for such wanderers to build a house, but they did what they could with low domes of brush where "the smoke could go out anywhere and the air could come in." They clothed their brown bodies only in a loincloth or a skirt of buckskin, browned by the desert dust to the color of an animal's hide. Even the moccasin, to the Whites the mark and sign of the Indian, they did not have. When they went on long journeys, they wove sandals of cactus fiber. Mostly, they went without any foot covering.

They made a few pots, of the red earth and rough as the desert floor. Dishes they reduced to two or three baskets, which did for eating, drinking, winnowing, even for cooking, if you shook the corn kernels in them with hot coals. Why multiply household utensils for the woman to carry on her back? It was a life stripped to essentials, unprotected as the animals. There was only one direction in which emotions could find a vent—in song.

But song was not simply self-expression. It was a magic which called upon the powers of Nature and constrained them to man's will. People sang in trouble, in danger, to cure the sick, to confound their enemies, and to make the crops grow. They sang, as they fought and as they worked, all together. This was a tiny, close-knit community, where the good of one was the good of all; where, if one person starved or was ill, the whole group suffered loss. So

A Papago home scene of a century ago

they gathered in villages, with a herald to tell them of approaching enemies. When one killed a deer, he divided it among them all. When the women dug wild roots, they gave just as much to her who stayed at home as to her who went. "How else could we keep alive?"

In such a community, song became not only the practical basis of Papago life, but also the most precious possession of the people. The power of song was an honor to be earned; it could not be assumed lightly at the mere whim of an individual. The describing of a desired event in the magic of beautiful speech was to them the means by which to make that event take place. All their songs describe such desired events, and besides the songs there are stately ritual orations intended for the same purpose. The songs are from every department of life and in many moods: solemn, wistful, humorous, wild. The mood does not matter. Magic will be worked if the description is vivid and if the singing or the recitation is done, as it should be, at the right time and with the right behavior, on behalf of all the people.

Such a magic spell is never consciously composed: it is "given" by the supernatural powers. A man who desired a song did not put his mind on words and tunes: he put it on pleasing the supernaturals. He must be a good hunter or a good warrior. Perhaps they would "like his ways" and one day, in a natural sleep, he would hear singing. So does the Papago interpret the trancelike state of the artist who derives his material from the unconscious. "He hears a song and he knows it is the hawk singing to him or the great white birds that fly from the ocean." Perhaps the clouds sing, or the wind, or the feathery red rain spider, swinging on its invisible rope.

A man who really longs for dreams does more than wait

and be industrious. There are Indians who bid such a man to fast and pray, but not the practical Papago; he asks the would-be singer to perform an act of heroism. The greatest of heroic acts is going to war, for the peaceful people have no delusions about the delight of battle. Battle is an ugly duty to be performed for the sake of one's kinsmen. There are other unwelcome duties of less need or honor in the present times, such as fetching salt from the one place where the Papagos find it, the waterless wastes that border the Gulf of California.

No man pretends that he delights in these hardships. Among the Papagos, bravery and repression of speech or emotion have no connection: when they feel fear or suffering, they say so. But this attitude of theirs does not prevent them from undergoing hardship as often as necessary. The reward is not personal glory, nor is it material riches, among a people who know no such things; the reward is dreams.

One who has performed an act of heroism has placed himself in contact with the supernatural. It is after this has been done, and not before, that he fasts and waits for a vision. The Papago sternly holds to the belief that visions do not come to the unworthy. But to the worthy man who shows himself humble there comes a dream. And a dream always contains a song.

To us, with our scheme wherein the singer stands outside the practical stream of life, and wherein he is thought of, perhaps even by most of us, as an idler, this philosophy is hardly comprehensible. Yet on it the Papago system of life has worked from time immemorial. The honored men are singers. The man who has fought for his people gets no honor from that fact, but only from the attendant fact that he was able to "receive"—or compose, shall we say—

a song. We who take the structure of our own society as a
sample of "human nature" might pause over this idea.
What of a society which puts no premium whatever on
aggressiveness and where the practical man is valued only
if he is also a poet? What of a society where the misfit,
wandering hopelessly misunderstood on the outskirts of
life, is not the artist, but the unimaginative young busi-
nessman? This society not only exists but has existed for
hundreds of years.

This volume presents those Papago songs that could be
culled from fourteen months of patient communion with
the old men. Since the songs are magic tools, it has not
seemed possible to present them without some description of the magic they are supposed to work. Such description is almost a part of the translation, for without it the
emotional weight of the songs could not be understood.

"Do they sing of spring?" a sympathetic friend asked
me. "Or of love?"

"No" to the first, for they have no spring. And to the
second, "Very little." Love works its own magic and needs
no song. It is only the sick and ungovernable who sing of
love, when they need to be cured of it. The songs deal
with the holiest of all things to the desert people, rain. To
them rain is endued with a life-giving loveliness: it is life
itself. The songs deal with the animals who flash to and fro
on the desert, at home in its ways as man can never be.
They deal with the springing beauty of the corn and they
speak almost with the amazed rapture that the birds and
animals might feel, had they found this means to make
food grow at their feet, instead of having to hunt for it
over the thirsting desert.

In describing the ceremonies, I do so in the present
tense. There has been a change, almost within a genera-

tion. People who went naked under the Arizona sun have put on the white man's clothing and built adobe houses. There are government wells in what was once the waterless desert, and government schools. But until the old men who knew the other ways are gone the core of the ancient life will remain. In some villages it is still intact; in some it is almost gone. Therefore the verbs of one describing Papago ways must shift continually between present and past. I have preferred to use the method of the old men who gave me the poetry and to draw the picture as though all of it were still to be found in the present.

THE PAPAGO BIBLE

HAVE INDIAN LANGUAGES any grammar? Is it true that their vocabularies contain no more than five hundred words? These questions beset one who mentions Indian poetry. Indian grammar is often more logical than our own, for people are not prone to remember strange forms with no dictionary to help them. As for the vocabulary, that question disappears after one has struggled to find a synonym for the noun meaning "the topmost feathers of an eagle's wing" or for the verb signifying "to sing in a harsh, croaking voice so that the words cannot be understood."

Papago songs are handed down from singer to singer more carefully than were the epics of Homer. A man dreams his own songs, and he gives them to his son; but before he was born, there was already a body of magic by which the ancestors ruled their world. This collected mass of song and story I have sometimes called the "Papago bible." Like much of the unwritten literature of our Southwest, it is half prose and half lyric in the manner of Aucassin and Nicolette. In that old French story, at every important crisis there is suddenly a song—an excellent device for sustaining interest and giving voice to the abbreviated emotional expression that suits a dramatic crisis. Few Indians make much use of the drama form, where the characters speak instead of being spoken about, but this device admirably takes its place and the songs are often in the first person, like a vivid soliloquy.

In every Papago village there is an old man whose he-

reditary function it is to recite this "bible." The accepted
time for the recitation is those four nights in winter "when
the sun stands still" before turning back from that southern journey which, it seemed, might take its light away
forever.

On those nights—four nights, for everything holy goes
by fours—the Papago men gathered in the ceremonial
house. One by one they puffed the ceremonial cigarette,
native tobacco in a hollow cane tube. Tobacco smoking
among the Papagos is like the burning of incense: a solemn function, not a recreation. Each man took four puffs,
then passed the cigarette sunwise, calling his neighbor by
the term of relationship. Of course they were all kin.
"Kinsman" and "neighbor" are the same word in Papago.

The men sat cross-legged, their arms folded, their heads
bowed. This was the position required by propriety, as
sitting upright in a church pew was required by our Vic-
torian ancestors. No one must interrupt the speaker by a
question or even by a movement. No one must doze. If
he did, some neighbor would poke the burning cigarette
between his sandaled toes. If the speaker saw it, he stopped
suddenly and there was no more storytelling that night.

The storyteller had, perhaps, worked years to memorize
the whole complicated mass of prose and verse. The prose
he sometimes elaborated with illustrations and explana-
tions of his own, but the verse was fixed. The words and
tune of every song were "given" by Elder Brother; also
the exact point where it entered the story. An old man
has refused to tell me a story because he had forgotten
the tune of one song and so was unable to tell the story
complete. Nevertheless, variations have crept in and the
"bible" according to one village is not quite that according to another.

The "Papago bible" would require a volume in itself and there are given here only the high lights of it, the songs. The narrative tells how the world was made by Earth-maker out of the dirt and sweat which he scraped from his skin. It tells how the flat earth met the sky with a crash like that of falling rocks, and from the two was born Iitoi, the protector of the Papagos. He had light hair and beard like that mysterious hero of the Toltecs, the culture-bringer Quetzalcoatl.

Iitoi and Earth-maker shaped and peopled the new world, and they were followed everywhere by Coyote, who came to life uncreated and began immediately to poke his nose into everything. In this new world there was a flood, and the three agreed before they took refuge that the one of them who should emerge first after the subsidence of the waters should be their leader and have the title of Elder Brother. It was Earth-maker, the creator, who came forth first, and Iitoi next, but Iitoi insisted on the title and took it. This usurper, displacing the misty figure of an older religion, is the hero of Papago myth.

Iitoi "brought the people up like children" and taught them their arts, but in the end he became unkind and they killed him. This happened, too, to Quetzalcoatl. It is an ancient theme in the Southwest: the theme of the dying god. With the Papagos and with some of the other tribes that tell this story, it does not point to hopelessness or to the idea that the unknown power is evil. We might read it so, but the Papago does not attribute to Iitoi the power of the Devil nor of God. He was the vessel through which power passed. And so are men. Power is impersonal, a great unknown force pervading the earth. It can be harnessed (to use a modern illustration) like an electric current, and used for anything, good or bad. Like the current, it is dangerous to him who uses it if he is not wise. The Papago understands how Iitoi could misuse it and how the medicine men can do so today.

But Iitoi, though killed, had so much power that he came to life again. Then he invented war. He decided to sweep from the earth the people he had made, and in order to do so he went through every act that the Papagos now go through when they decide to chastise an enemy. He needed an army and for this purpose he went underground and brought up the Papagos. It is thus that they explain their origin. They live in a land scattered with imposing ruins which belonged, according to them, to the Hohokam, "the people who are gone." Archaeologists are still hunting for these vanished people, who built the Casa Grande, five stories high. The Papagos know where they went: Iitoi drove them, some to the north and some to the south. We may conjecture whether they are to be found mingled with the present Pueblos of New Mexico and Arizona or confounded with peoples of the almost obliterated cultures of ancient Mexico. The Papagos, to whom geography beyond their own mountains is unimportant, do not go into that; but they know what battle was fought at each of those mysterious ruins and they know that the actual conquest came through singing: "Iitoi had a song for everything." Though his men did the fighting, Iitoi confirmed their efforts by singing the enemy into blindness and helplessness. So he laid the foundations for the Papago world.

This is the story which is told at the winter solstice and forbidden in summer, the season of the profane. Men who wish to make magic for war, for hunting, or for any act of life will learn some of Iitoi's songs from listening year by year or by begging them from the singer. But men who

have really dreamed will make their own. For hundreds
of years the Papagos have been doing this, until the songs
for any kind of magic mount into the thousands. Iitoi has
retired from the world and lives, a little old man, in a
mountain cave. Or, perhaps, he has gone underground.
The warm, safe ground has for many Indians the attrac-
tion that the sky has for us. They see the sky in some very
evil moods and they sometimes look with more envy at
the badger who digs than at the hawk who flies.

The songs which constrain Nature have often the brief,
brilliant accuracy of the Chinese. All that is necessary to
make their magic prevail is a description of the desired
thing. The singer need not employ the lofty phraseology
of prayer. He can let his imagination play with the picture of the spotted deer, drinking from the water hole in
the rock, where the white flowers grow. He can see the
brown crickets chirping at the foot of the corn and the
dragonfly darting hither and thither. He may even laugh
at these homely and beloved things, for "it does not matter if you laugh or if you scold, just so you make them
real." Such is our own dictum in the making of poetry.
Though our magic influences only the world within, and
the Papagos', the world without, the rules which both have
arrived at are the same.

Besides the songs, there is spoken poetry. In fact, a ceremony comprises, as with many other peoples, a recitation
by the priest and hymns by the multitude. These recitations are no longer dreamed. They have been "given" to
certain old men, who pass them down to their male heirs.
But never ask a Papago what "given" means. You will
only receive the answer, "So it is." For centuries these ancient orations have been handed down and some of their
phrases parallel phrases in the Aztec prayers to Aztec gods.

But they are not prayers. They are, like the songs, descriptions of desired events. They are told in the first person as though the speaker himself had lived through them. Many must have been the young men, aflame with a vague sense of the glory of life, whose imaginative images were crystallized in these terms and whose dreams were of the things the first singer had seen, as our poets still dream of the fairies invented by another age.

These ancient orations have certain fixed and beautiful phrases which seemed so magic-working that there was no need ever to change them. On some subjects, indeed, there arose a magic language in which the metaphors always remained the same. The sun was "the shining traveler," Coyote was "our furry comrade, our burning-eyed comrade." We are not unfamiliar with this habit, for we have but to remember "the blue-eyed Achaeans" of Homer, and "the sea, the swan road" of Beowulf.

One real difference there is between the Indian sense of beauty and our own: we can have enough of repetition; the Indian, apparently, can not. Often these Papago poems skip from one point of high emotion to another with amazing brevity: the most modern impressionist could ask no more. But if there begins some magic experience which can happen four times, then four times it must happen, even though it be pages—or, for the Indian, hours—long. Therefore in this book some of the repetitions have been omitted. The reader may imagine them.

But no other violence has been done. A translator of a language so different from ours in all its devices as is an Indian tongue has much to answer for. The entire way of thought is different. So are the grammatical forms and the order of words. One can hope to make the translation exact only in spirit, not in letter; yet I have striven for literal accuracy. The form which has emerged is, to my surprise, very like that of our own Early English ballads. This came about not from a desire for mere picturesqueness. The Papago has a verb form with a past auxiliary which can be best translated by our old word "did." "Then did he swiftly go" is an exact translation of Papago form and Papago word order. In the same way, our old expressions, "to me-ward," "his horse beside," are literal Papago. I did not employ these, because there is a limit to the obsolete expressions one may use if the reading is to be easy. But "therewith," "thereon," "thereby," seemed not too ancient to be allowable. A Papago would also say "him-with, him-to," but, again, there is a limit.

A Papago sentence has a definite word order in which everything is packed in before the verb, somewhat as it is in German; everything, that is, but the subject—which comes last. The following sentence may give some idea of the arrangement:

"Then did he yonder immediately to him-ward
swiftly go, that youth."

There is a beauty and a rhythm in the arrangement which we can appreciate; but we could hardly read sentence after sentence in that order without weariness and without forgetting what it was all about, and therefore I have only suggested the idea where it could be done easily. If it sounds like an imitation of the classics, I have but to apologize to the Papagos, for they worked out the system for themselves, and I only wish I could render it better.

The songs, meant to be sung, have other untranslatable qualities. Indian languages have no rhyme. Usually they have not that essential for rhyme, a number of synonyms. One word means one thing, and sometimes the thing is as definite as the-two-top-feathers-of-an-eagle's-wings. There-fore there can be little juggling with words. But Indian songs have rhythm. It is not the regular rhythm of our verses or our musical bars—all the same, like marching steps. It is a much more complicated and varied arrange-ment, in which the tempo may change with every phrase. But with the words and the word order fixed, what jug-gling is possible, even with rhythm? The poet takes things into his own hands and simply adds an extra syllable to the word or cuts one out. The result is a singer's language, which the listeners may not even understand. One who is writing down songs must first write them as sung, then as spoken, then the translation.

Papago has rules, even for this. There are certain sorts of syllables which fit certain words, other which do not. The reasons are onomatapoetic: they have to do with the sound of the word and its fitness to convey a feeling. It is an art halfway between poetry and music and one for which our own activities have no parallel. But I could quote a modern Papago song describing a railway train jolting over the rails in front of the singer, then roaring away in the distance. As it jolts, the added syllables are full of harsh consonants. As it vanishes, there are only *m*'s and a word which really ends with *m* has been chosen for the final verb. This branch of Indian art is a real contri-bution. It cannot be translated in full. But the sensitive ears which find it absolutely necessary that a word should express the speaker's feeling in sound as well as in mean-ing may bring something new to our own poetry.

The ceremonies to which these songs and this poetry belonged must be imagined now, not seen. The Papagos keep to their old ways more than do any other Indians in the country, except the Pueblos. But they had no beau-

tiful panoply of color to accompany their singing, as had
the people of the mesas. The beauty of the ceremony came
from the loneliness of the naked figures against the stark
desert. Blue jeans, calico dresses, and the waiting automobiles of the Whites make them look pathetic. Yet they
are majestic. Therefore I have felt that their words, holding both sound and meaning and containing much of that
majesty, should be preserved.

THE DRINKING RITUAL

"DO THE WHITES NOT UNDERSTAND," an old Papago said to me, "that we have no water except what comes from the sky? We have no canned food, so we need the corn to feed our children. We have no automobiles, so we need hay for our horses. Why then do they say we should not drink the cactus liquor?"

The making and drinking of the cactus liquor is Papago rain magic. It is made from the fruit of the giant cactus (*Cereus giganteus*), a unique American plant found only in our Southwest and in Mexico. Those who have seen its stark columns marching over the southern hillsides never forget its grotesque formation, as much like marble or plaster as an organic growth. The shafts, thick and tall as tree trunks, have, instead of bark, a green pulp, fluted like an Ionic column, its perpendicular ridges set with long, white thorns, in clumps of three. Sometimes the shafts extrude strange branches, curving like the arms of a starfish. The pulp, in the rainy season, has the patina of jade-green tile; in the dry season, of yellow-brown brick. The thorns, as the seasons wax and wane, change from new white, which catches the sun like a halo, to wilted brown. The entire column is a reservoir of water whose flutings contract in the dry season and expand in the rains.

Upon its top, stemless, like perching birds, grow the figlike fruits which produce the liquor. They ripen just at the end of the dry season and it is no wonder that their juice is thought to be the prototype of the coming rain.

Mixed with water, it ferments in two days to a gentle, musty-tasting cider. Perhaps beer would be a more appropriate name to give to the drink, for it has a low alcoholic content.

It is the duty of every man to drink his fill of this liquor; to drink to a saturation, even as the rain-soaked earth is saturated. In accordance with the rules of Papago magic, which always imitates the desired event, this act will bring the rain to moisten the earth.

The ancient Aztecs, too, had such a belief. With them, drinking was a holy ritual permitted only to the old men, and a young man who drank was punished with death. The Papagos have a gentler rule which permits all men to drink, and even sometimes women. But it is only on one occasion. The cider keeps its intoxicating quality for a few hours only, and while it is in this magic state, every drop must be consumed.

Giant
cactus

In the old days there was no more drinking until next year. It must be confessed that the Whites, who have taught the Indian that smoking is not an act of worship but a daily pleasure, have also encouraged him to drink whenever he has money instead of only when he wants to "pull down the clouds." But the solemn ceremony of drinking, with song and oratory, is still practiced in many villages in the form that was "given" by Elder Brother. I, who have seen it often, have never seen the intoxication lead to anything more violent than song.

The giant cactus clusters on the southern hillsides away from the villages, and there every family has a hereditary grove where it goes to camp under a thatched shelter. Each June they arrive and dig from its hiding place a huge cooking jar in which to boil the fruit. Every day

the women go out at sunrise, for cactus picking is women's
work. Each carries a long rod, slender as a fishing pole,
with little transverse sticks tied along it with cactus fibers,
and with this she hooks the fruit down from the thorny
shafts, twenty-five feet high. Perhaps it breaks as it falls
and displays a pulp like that of a crimson fig; or she splits
it with her fingernail, throws the pulp into her basket,
and leaves the halves of the shell lying on the ground, the
red side uppermost to "summon the rain."

When the ten-o'clock sun beats down unbearably, the
women return to the shelter and dump their bushels of
juicy pulp into the cooking pot. It is not juice alone that
the cactus provides. When the juice is boiled, and strained
through a basket, there is still a pulp, one of the few sweets
known to the Papagos, and there are the oily seeds which
supply both grease and flour. In late afternoon the second
gathering expedition is made, and thus the syrup jar grows
full. At night the old men who are the singers of a Papago
village come out from the shelter and lie under the stars
to sing. And listening, the boys learn the drinking songs,
without which no man should receive a drink.

At last the jar is full and the first scattering raindrops
indicate that the dry season is at an end. The families
come trooping to the village in the plains and bring their
contribution to the huge jars in the council house. They
are received by the man appointed by the village for this
duty, who is called "He-Who-Desires-Liquor." He pours
the crimson juice into a jar and measures the quantity of
water which must go with it. Sometimes he has an ancient
man to help him, known as "Thin Lips" or "Squirrel
Lips" because his sensitive lips can tell when the mixture
is right.

A little fire is built so that for seventy-two hours the

liquor may ferment in even warmth. The old men must sit beside it to sing, lest any magic influence it, and outside the people must sing it into fermentation. Two nights of song is the regular measure, and the crier calls all the people:

> Our fire has burned and the sun has gone down;
> Our fire has burned and the sun has gone down.
> Come together, following our ancient custom.
> Sing for the liquor,
> Delightfully sing.

From all the houses the black figures emerge in the starlight to go to the dance place outside the council house. The "rain house" is its name for this occasion when it fulfills its most sacred function. Against its wall sit the old men who know the songs. Above their heads is strung the sacred line of eagle feathers, hardly discernible against the black sky. In the center of the dance place is a tiny fire, for a large one would "frighten away the clouds." Beside the fire the medicine man lights his cigarette and puffs slowly, watching to see when the rain may be expected. Before the nights of singing are over, he will know.

The delicate crepitation of a rattle is heard—tiny pebbles shaken inside a hollow gourd. The chief singer has come. He leans toward the old men to get his instructions, and then his voice sounds in a harsh cry, almost like that of a bird—the first phrases of a song. Instantly dark forms have joined him, men in cowboy hats and high-heeled boots stepping sidewise around the fire. They have not completed one of the sixteen repetitions which ceremony demands before the women also come stealing through the darkness. This is a night when a woman has her choice of partners. She watches the line of men tramp by and

While the liquor ferments

suddenly the silhouette of the desired one appears. He need not be her husband. Love has no laws tonight, and many new matings have their beginning under the eagle feathers. She gathers her shawl about her, parts the hands of two men, and takes her place between them.

More women come and more men until the circle includes a hundred people or more. Over their shoulders the medicine man can be seen walking to and fro and holding up eagle plumes to catch the wind. Sometimes, if he has great magic, he can sprinkle drops from his plumes upon the dancers. Until morning they sing songs of rain and cloud, of the little red spiders and the little gray horned toads who are the friends of the rain, and of the frogs who are its messengers.

SONGS TO PULL DOWN THE CLOUDS

The sun is setting,
The mountain shadow
Covers me and stretches on.
In front of the great mountain
Darkness comes forth
And speedily it moves.

———

The sun children
Are running westward
Hand in hand,
Madly singing,
Running.

———

Where stands the cloud, trembling
On Quijotoa Mountain,
The cloud trembling,
There lies my heart
Trembling.

———

Within Quijotoa Mountain
There is thunder.
I looked through it and saw
In every direction
Light!

———

Wind came, clouds came.
I sat above them.
Underneath, the mirage glittered.
Rain fell,
The mirage was gone.

The little red spiders
And the little gray horned toad
Together they make the rain to fall;
They make the rain to fall.

———

Upon the Children's Land
The waters run and overflow,
Upon the Stream-bed Mountain
The waters run and overflow.

———

Corn is forming,
Corn is forming.
Beside it, squash is forming.
In the yellow flowers
The flies sing.

———

At the edge of the world
It is growing light.
The trees stand shining.
I like it.
It is growing light.

———

At the edge of the world
It is growing light.
Up rears the light.
Just yonder the day dawns,
Spreading over the night.

MOCKINGBIRD SPEECHES

THE TWO NIGHTS of fermentation by song are over. In the heat of morning, tired people lie sleeping on the gravel before the adobe houses. But two men have not slept. They are the messengers whose duty it is to call the neighbor villages to the feast, and before dawn they mount their horses, or, in the old days, plod away through the dark on their woven sandals. Each is assigned to a particular village, where an official awaits him in front of the council house.

They are no impromptu words that he speaks. The invitation to the Sit-and-Drink was "given" in the unknown past, in magic words that help to bring the rain.

> Am not I a messenger
> Desiring a delightful thing?
>
> Once I knew not what to do
> To make the liquor.
> At the foot of a tree, prone I lay.
> The wind blew.
> Dust it blew along the ground
> And cast it in my face.
> Twigs it blew along the ground
> And tangled them in my hair.
>
> Then I arose.
> Of the kinsmen living around me I
>   bethought me
> And they had pity on me.

Some liquid in the bottom of a jar
They gave me.
Crouching, I sat before it,
Desiring that speedily it should ferment.
But still it did not.

Then it had pity on me
And, after two mornings,
Gloriously it fermented.

Then of those whose desires were like
    to mine
I bethought me,
And straight to you a shining road was
    stretched.
As I started upon it,
It was the wind that met me
And rainily it blew.
It was this that I desired in what I did.

As again I started upon it,
It was cloudiness that met me
And soft rain sprinkled.
It was this that I desired in what I did.

Then came I to your sacred house and
    saw.
All kinds of winds there lay,
All kinds of clouds there lay,
All kinds of seeds there lay.
Seated upon them was One who power-
    fully touched you.
He swayed to and fro and blew out his
    breath.

Then came I to my sacred house and saw.
All kinds of winds there lay,
All kinds of clouds there lay,
All kinds of seeds there lay.
Seated upon them was One who power-
          fully touched me.
He blew out his winds and his clouds.

He pressed against me
And left me moistened and healed.
Then came forth the growing things.
Therewith were delightful the evenings,
Delightful the dawns.

Then hurry and, in any way you can,
Come swallow my fermented liquor.

This is the Mockingbird Speech, so called because the
mockingbird is the most eloquent of birds and can
"stretch his words like ropes between the mountaintops."
The invited village has also its mockingbird speaker, who
responds in a dignified antiphony, almost repeating the
words of his host. Then he and his village march to the
rendezvous.

That scene is more brilliant now than in the old days
of half-naked people in skins and undyed cotton, their
chief ornament their flowing black hair. No one wore
anything above the waist in the old days, and they painted
their bodies as gaily as they could, the women with birds
and butterflies, sometimes different for each breast. The
young dandies reddened the soles of their feet so that
when they fell over, drunk, the beautiful color would
show.

Now the men appear in all the gorgeousness of cowboy shirts—magenta, emerald green, blazing yellow. Their black eyes gleam under cowboy hats, their horses wear every scrap of stamped silver available. The women are swathed in mantillas of peacock blue, crimson, and pink. It is late morning and the desert sunshine pours on the colors in blinding brilliance.

The men form a circle outside the sacred rain house, while the women stand aside under its porch. This is the Sit-and-Drink, as the native language has it, the occasion when the liquor will be ceremonially consumed, with ritual recitations which must bring rain. Everyone is wild with expectation, both of the liquor, which is drunk but once a year (or used to be), and of the rain, which will make life easy again. But there is solemn decorum, for this is a religious ceremony. Here, before the baskets of liquor go round, are recited some of the most beautiful of the descriptions of rain and fruitfulness. The more satisfying the description, the more satisfying will be the rain it brings.

INVITATION TO BE SEATED IN THE DRINKING CIRCLE

[*The Mockingbird Orator addresses this speech in turn to the heads of all visiting villages. The man addressed is then carried on the shoulders of his hosts and seated at the side of the circle corresponding geographically to the position of his village.*]

But now did I come to you as messenger, friend,
Desiring a delightful thing.

Some little things I planted in my field,
Crawling on hands and knees
With my weed hoe.
Nothing could I raise
That would ferment.

Only my child knew the plants
That were around us.
Repeatedly did he go picking them,
And in the palm of my hand he placed them.
With water I mixed them;
Crouching before the jar I sat,
Desiring that speedily it should ferment.
After two mornings it felt kindly toward me
And gloriously it fermented.

Then did I think of the medicine men
Wherever they might be living,
And here a shining road did stretch and reach
        to you.
Where I set forth
It was my wind that blew rainily.
Where I set forth again,
It was my cloudiness
That sprinkled moistly.
It was this that I desired in what I did.

To you I came.
I saw that at the base of your brush house
Much moisture stood.
From under it the water in short streams ran,
It pleased me.
Into a long narrow bundle I made it and I
        took it.
Behind you I looked.
I saw that for the heads of your mountains
The mist made circlets.
Beneath them the earth lay green with moisture.
It pleased me.
Into a long narrow bundle I made it and I
        took it.

I turned me back again.
I reached my sacred house.
I saw that at the base of my brush house
Much moisture stood.
From under it the water in short streams ran.
Therewith for the heads of the mountains
      around me
The mist made circlets.

In that [mist] for you the red liquor
I dipped and poured;
I, having drunk, gave to you;
I drew you forward and set you in the circle.
You swallowed and were gloriously drunk.
Then was I not ungenerous with beautiful
      speech
And with beautiful singing.
Thus, vying together, we made an end.

Then did I go gathering up the remains of
      the feast
And to my former camping place I went;
I lay down.
The remains of the feast did I leave here
And again in my former camping place did
      I lie down.
There, after two mornings, a wind arose,
Well knowing whither it should blow.
On the place of our feasting did it beautifully
      rain,
As much as was needed.

Hurry, come and drink my fermented liquor!

It is time to drink, and within the council house the liquor is ready, in great watertight willow baskets. But this is a sacred feast and, before the first drop is taken, He-Who-Desires-Liquor comes forward to make a speech of admonition:

"I have made this liquor that you may drink and be happy. Very beautifully you will get drunk. Very happily you will get drunk. Let no one be angry: let no one raise his hand to strike. If someone comes from a distance, keep watch of his horse for him. Tie the horse; put the saddle in your house; put the bridle in your house; put the spurs in your house. When he comes to himself, wherever he may be, he will take his horse; he will take his saddle; he will take his bridle; his spurs he will take. So he will come happily to his home and happy will be the Liquor-maker."

From the rain house, four cupbearers bring four baskets containing the thick, dark-crimson liquor. They take it to the four visitors, at north, south, east, and west. Then each basket moves round the circle counterclockwise. As the cupbearer dips for each man, he hails him by the kinship term, says: "Drink, friend. Grow beautifully drunk."

The baskets are exhausted. Before they can be replenished, there must be singing and more calling upon the clouds. The Mockingbird Speaker advances again. A younger man, who is his witness and pupil, leads him by the hand. They stand before the visitor at the east and the Mockingbird Speaker addresses him:

> Ready, friend!
> Are we not here drinking
> The shaman's drink,
> The magician's drink!
> We mix it with our drunken tears and drink.

See yonder the ceremonial house that stands
    within the east!
Within it hangs a white-winged mockingbird.
Four times with inverted head he spoke,
Straight down descending spoke;
Thus here he moistened the earth.

Yonder at the edge of the earth a wind swayed
    to and fro,
Well knowing whither it should move.
The standing trees it went shaking;
The rubbish at the foot of the trees it went
    piling high.
Over toward the west it went, and back it
    turned.
It saw the earth lie beautifully smoothed and
    finished.

Above emerged a huge white cloud.
With its head against the sky it stood;
Then it began to move.
Although the earth seemed very wide,
Clear to the edge of it it went.

From within the great rainy mountains
Rushed out a huge black cloud
And joined with it.
Pulling out their white breast feathers they went;
Spreading their white breast feathers far and
    wide they went;
Then they stood still and saw.

Although the ditches lying side by side
Thought they could carry the flow
With little effort,
Full to the brim they were
And choked with rubbish piled crosswise.
Although the flood channels lying side by side
Thought they could carry the flow
With little effort,
Full to the brim they were
And choked with rubbish piled crosswise.

Clear to the west went [the clouds]
And back they turned them.
They saw the earth lie beautifully moist and
  finished.
Upon it came forth seed;
And a thick root came forth,
And a thick stalk came forth;
Great broad leaves came forth,
And well they ripened.
Therewith were delightful the evenings,
Delightful the dawns.

Let us all but desire this one end.
If thus we do, we shall see it.

The man addressed responds with a song, solemnly
sung in slow rhythm:

   Am not I medicine man!
   I cause the wind to run.
   My elder brother the land,
    it floods with water.

Am not I a doughty man!
I cause the cloud to fly.
My younger brother the mountain,
    it washes with water.

Just yonder a cloud comes forth;
And here it trembles,
Softly thundering.

Just yonder a mist grows long;
And here it trembles,
Softly drizzling.

They make me drink the cup:
Here I cause the wind to blow;
Red spiders run on the field.

They make me drink the cup:
Here I cause the cloud to fly;
The centipede walks on the field.

So the ceremony proceeds, with solemn words and with
solemn singing, to its conclusion.

COVERING THE WINE WITH SONG

THE CIRCLE around the rain house has broken up. Each household goes plodding home in the blinding noon sunshine to where its own jar of liquor has been buried to ferment in the even warmth of the earth.

"I put you here," the housewife said as she buried it; for the Papagos always speak to natural objects with which they deal, like members of a family who explain their acts so that all may remain friends. "I put you here. Do you ferment and make good liquor."

Now it has fermented—or if not, there has been witchcraft somewhere. The family is at home for the day as in our onetime New Year's celebration, and all their friends come calling. At least, they come until the liquor is exhausted. Then a shout from the other end of the village announces that some other jar has reached the peak of fermentation, and all the bright shirts and the galloping horses are off in that direction.

The host holds in his hand a gourd cup. He dips it into the brownish red liquor and hands it to a guest. "Friend, be beautifully drunk." The guest swallows in one draft, but he would not be so rude as to return the cup until he has "covered it with a song."

There are thousands of such songs, both the old ones sung at the first liquor feast and the new ones dreamed every year. Few men have never dreamed a song, and in fact it would be a dull man who could not put together the sacred words of "cloud," "rain," and "corn" in some form he could call his own. But the born poets or dreamers go farther and make pictures of the shining red spiders on adobe, gleaming with wet, or the mountain where a cloud catches. They hymn the glories of dizziness. The words which mean "drunken" and "dizzy" are, in the Papago language, sacred and poetic words, for the trance of drunkenness is akin to the trance of vision.

> Dizziness is following me!
> Close it is following me.
> Ah, but I like it.
> Yonder far, far
> On the flat land it is taking me.
>
> Dizziness I see.
> High up there I see it.
> Truly I like it.
> Yonder they lead me.
> And dizziness they give me to drink.
>
> 'Tis at the foot of little Gray Mountain
> I am sitting and getting drunk.
> Beautiful songs I shall unfold.
>
> The little playful women,
> The little playful women,
> Whence got they dizziness?
> Therewith they made my heart drunk.
> The little playful women,
> When they are dizzy
> Surely they will take me.

Dizzy women
Are seizing my heart.
Westward they are leading me.
I like it.
One on each side,
They are leading me.

Much dizziness,
Much dizziness
Within me is swelling,
And more and more.
Every which way I am falling.

SINGING UP THE CORN

As soon as the liquor has been drunk, there come lightnings at the south, and then the windstorm, "bearing the rain on its back." It is late July, the moon of rain. The desert riots with purple vetch and yellow rabbit brush, with the huge moons of white poppies and the flame-points of pink starflowers. Now planting can begin.

Every man has his field at the mouth of a wash where the water comes down after the rains in a swirling red torrent. It floods the land for half a day till the desert sun has sucked it up and the dead dry soil has sucked it down. Then the ground is soft enough for the Papago to thrust into it a sharp-pointed stick which was once his only spade. He stands at the edge of the field, holding his digging stick and a buckskin pouch of corn kernels. Kneeling, he makes his hole and speaks to the seed, in the Papago manner of explaining all acts to Nature lest there be misunderstanding: "Now I place you in the ground. You will grow tall. Then they shall eat, my children and my friends who come from afar."

Carefully he makes the holes, one at each stride, and drops in four corn kernels, and behind him his woman covers the holes with her bare toes. Now the corn will come up "like a feather headdress" and the beans will come "singing together." But not without help. Night after night, the planter walks around his field "singing up the corn." There is a song for corn as high as his knee, for corn waist high, and for corn with the tassel forming. Sometimes, all the men of a village meet together and sing all night, not only for the corn but also for the beans, the squash, and the wild things. They make effigies contrived cunningly out of wood and leaves, for the Papago had few possessions except those supplied by Nature. Sitting in a circle before their rude imitations of the fruits of the earth, the men sang.

Evening is falling.
Pleasantly sounding
Will reverberate
Our songs.

———

The corn comes up;
It comes up green;
Here upon our fields
White tassels unfold.

The corn comes up;
It comes up green;
Here upon our fields
Green leaves blow in the breeze.

———

Blue evening falls,
Blue evening falls;
Near by, in every direction,
It sets the corn tassels trembling.

———

The wind smooths well the ground.
Yonder the wind runs
Upon our fields.
The corn leaves tremble.

Using the weed hoe

On Tecolote fields
The corn is growing green.
I came there, saw the tassels waving in
    the breeze,
And I whistled softly for joy.

———

Blowing in the wind,
Singing,
Am I crazy corn?

Blowing in the wind,
Singing,
Am I laughing corn?

[Corn with kernels of two colors is called "crazy corn"; when there are three colors, it is "laughing corn."]

The night moves, singing.
Not sleepy, I.
A stick I cut to represent the corn.
Where I find the yellow bees
There will be much corn.

———

A little yellow cricket
At the roots of the corn
Is hopping about and singing.

A little yellow cricket
At the roots of the squash
Is hopping about and singing.

———

[*Corn speaks:*]
The little striped woodpecker
Descends right down into my heart.

[*Man speaks:*]
This my bow
Twangs in the cornfield.

———

It moves in different directions,
It moves in different directions,
And then it alights
From the south,
On the blue water—
The dragonfly.

It moves in different directions,
It moves in different directions,
And then it stands still
From the south,
On the yellow water—
The dragonfly.

All together, all together they sing—
The red beans.
All together, all together they sing—
The white beans.

Am I not the magic tobacco?
Here I come forth and grow tall.
Am I not the magic tobacco?
The blue hummingbird finds my flowers.
Above them softly he is humming.

At last they sing the harvest song, as the corn of different colors speaks from the harvester's arms.

Truly most comfortably you embrace me:
I am the blue corn.
Truly most comfortably you embrace me:
I am the red corn.

THE ANIMALS, OUR SUPERIORS

THE IDEA OF BEING KIND to animals belongs to a race which looks down on them from a lofty height. To the Papago, and to most other Indians, this would be laughable. It is the animals who should be kind to man, for they are more at home on the earth than he. They know how to live on friendly terms with the land without being always too hot, too cold, or too hungry.

A starving man hardly thought of kindness when he looked at the light and tireless woodpecker, crested in a scarlet he had never achieved, extracting its food from the dry trunks of trees. When he sat in his drafty hut, in terror of a skulking enemy, he thought of the badger, housed warm and safe beneath the stifling earth. He thought with reverence, for the animals had power.

It is true that man kills the animals for his food and clothing, but this is only with their own consent. They are willing to offer their bodies for death—which is not real death, because after it they go back to their secret kingdom and take bodies again. In fact, the animal body is put on at will in order to be more comfortable in the world. Animals could act and talk like man if they cared to, and it is the aim of every man to win the friendship of some animal who will so talk to him and teach him swiftness and sagacity. Some day, when he lies exhausted on the desert after thirty miles of running, a badger or a hawk may stand beside him singing. It will sing of its own habits, and whatever it tells brings power, even if the visitant is only the wise little ant who knows how to make a home in the empty sand. Its song means magic. The man who has met an animal bears as a title of honor the name: Hawk-meeter, Wildcat-meeter, Ant-meeter.

Just as they give power, the animals send disease. It is their vengeance on the human beings who have not understood their ways. If anyone has killed an animal which he did not need for food, it is a sin which that animal will punish with illness. If he has made the animal suffer by an unskilled arrow shot or even if he has shown disrespect to its bones by leaving them where the dogs may drag them about, he will suffer. He sickens and sends for the medicine man, who comes, gazes into his crystal, and says, "This is the owl disease [or, the bat disease; or, the deer disease]." No one can cure it but those who have "met the owl [or, the bat; or, the deer]," and these specialists must be sent for, from no matter how far away. Each knows songs describing the habits of the particular visitant and using that powerful magic, the mention of his name.

The songs, like all Papago magic, are not prayers. They are only descriptions, and it does not matter whether they praise or ridicule. They may even show downright disrespect, for men with a touch of humor are often wont to dream in comic style. The point is to visualize the animal with all the peculiarities which are to evoke him and make him real. Thus his power is asserted and he is willing to revoke the punishment of disease. In these animal songs the accuracy of Papago gift for observation is seen at its best. They are little vignettes of desert life, humorous, exquisite, and friendly. "The animal does not mind how one speaks of him if one makes people understand what he is."

Animal visitants are described
in song

Quail children under the bushes
Were chattering.
Our comrade Coyote heard them.
Softly he came padding up
And stood wriggling his ears
In all directions.

Our comrade Coyote, thirsty,
Just yonder lay down to sleep.
Quail birds above him
Fluttered their wings.
Frightened, he jumped up and
        looked about him.
Haiya, God my father!
Would it might rain, now!

———

A lizard maiden
Was thirsty and crying.
A gila monster ran up
And comforted her.
The maiden stopped crying.
The monster carried her off
And took her to wife.

A little gray horned toad medicine man
Lost his wife.
All over the earth he ran
Sorrowing.

———

[*The owl speaks:*]
Just before me
The evening is growing red.
I fly out and four times
I hoot.

[*The eagle speaks:*]
The sun's rays
Lie along my wings
And stretch beyond their tips.

Little black turtle
Medicine man!
Over there crawling, crawling, crawling!
Over there crawling!

———

A little black turtle
Just yonder at Pitcikin
Was drunk and was ogling the girls;
Trying to talk Mexican,
Trying to talk English;
"For I am so bright!"
Said the turtle.

———

A little gray whirlwind
Is trying to catch me.
Across my path
It keeps whirling.

THE HEAD-BEARERS

WHEN THE PAPAGOS first came up from the underworld, Elder Brother made them the deer for their food and clothing. But it was to be more than that. Because the deer was the first food, deer flesh has curative powers. The first deer of the season must be cooked with singing, and the people all crowd up for a mouthful, each begging it, "Give me life." The plumy deer tail, the symbol of the animal, has become a magic property. It is given as an offering to the enemy scalps. It is laid out reverently under the stars on the night when the liquor must ferment. The words that indicate rich offerings are "eagle down," "deer tails," and "beads."

To make the deer, Elder Brother first took a squirrel and slit it up the middle. But the squirrel cried, so he set it down. It bears only a white mark on its underpart to show what it might have been. Then he took a desert mouse. Though it was small, it did not cry; so he slit it and made the deer.

He "gave it the wind as its friend," to tell of human approach. He gave it ears that hear the earth vibrate under human footsteps. He gave it no gall bladder (hunters who butcher the deer have observed this fact), so that it never felt anger. But also he gave it "to know when its time was come." Then the deer voluntarily approaches the hunter and waits to be killed.

Head-bearers, the hunters are called, because they wear a deer-head disguise. Mounting it on his head, each creeps on all fours to leeward of the grazing deer. But to have such a headdress and to know how to use it means an apprenticeship from boyhood on. Deer hunting is the most skilled of all Papago crafts.

A boy who wants to be a head-bearer approaches some old man and asks for instruction. "Are you sure you want

The deer hunter

to do this?" asks the elder. "It is a hard life. You must run on the mountains without food. You must stay away from the village month after month." If the boy persists that he wants to learn, the old man begins at the very beginning by showing him how to make arrows. It will be months or years before he can properly chip the hard stone, straighten the reed shafts, and attach the feathers.

During these years, he carries arrows for the adult head-bearers, ready to rush forward with the quiver if the enemy is sighted instead of the deer; ready to help move the deer's head to the west when a kill has been made. For

the deer is not killed lightly: every step in the process is
"given."

At last he kills a deer of his own. He must not eat a
mouthful of it, for this would spoil his luck as a hunter.
He presents it to his teacher, and out of it his own deer-
head disguise is made. Now he is invited to go to the hills
with the other head-bearers. In their pouches they take
white chalk to color their bronzed arms and legs to the
shade of the deer. They wear buckskin, white in front and
black with soot on the back; for the deer will not be too
discerning if it sees only some four-legged animal with
black back and white underside.

They carry the heavy masks and climb to some woody
hill far from the flat lands where the villages are planted.
Perhaps they take with them a medicine man with the
crystal which allows him to "see" where the deer will be.
As they climb into the hills, they do not speak; for noise
always seems, to the Papago, to be disrespectful to the supernatural powers. They settle silently around the campfire to stir and drink their few mouthfuls of corn-meal
gruel. Then they sing the deer to them. There are series
of songs dreamed by ancient hunters who were always successful, which tell of the deer's haunts and habits; for the
more closely the deer is portrayed, the more surely the
songs bring him toward them. Some of the songs are sung
by the flowers on which the deer browses, and some by the
deer itself; for "the deer can dream and sing songs like
a man."

They sing for half the night. Rest preceding effort is
no part of Papago philosophy, and a man preparing to
fight or hunt feels himself stronger after wakefulness or
fasting. When at last they lie back to sleep, the deer, in
the form of a beautiful woman, comes in dreams and

makes a rendezvous for the next day. When the hunter kills the deer there, he lays its head to the westward and speaks reverently: "Now do not make me ill because I have killed you. You were left here for that purpose, that I might kill you and that I might eat you." He takes home the deer tail as his most cherished possession and he distributes the meat among all his neighbors according to Papago economy. The neighbors will give him something when they can, and, if not, "he would do it anyway; how else could they eat?"

At last the hunter begins to dream his own songs, for even this skilled craft finds its culmination in singing. The songs here given were collected from many head-bearers and arranged by the translator.

[*The hunter:*]
The deer is spotted,
On the flat land he goes running.
The deer is spotted,
On the mountains he goes running.
These my hands I cover with white
    clay
And on the ground I creep.

———

[*The deer:*]
Here a little moisture
Is dripping.
Here grows the white datura by
    the water.
Here a little moisture
Is dripping.

[*The datura:*]
The lizard weed is like me,
It has yellow blossoms.

———

[*The lizard weed:*]
The datura is like me,
It has white blossoms.

———

[*The deer:*]
Bird children—
There by my singing place
They chatter low and sing.

Bird children—
There by my standing place
They chatter low and run away.

———

[*The hunter:*]
The red ocotillo flower—
There I found the deer;
They ran,
They broke it down.

The yellow chamiso flower—
There I found the deer;
They rushed forth,
They broke it down.

———

The mountain gap—
Thither the deer run climbing;
Beyond it the reeds
They scatter and break.

The mountain ridge—
Thither the deer run circling;
Beneath it the reeds
They scatter and break.

————

[*The deer:*]
The wind is rushing toward us
Far off,
Turning somersaults as it comes.
At the edge of the world
It stands still.

The clouds are coming toward us
Near by,
Spreading out as they come.
On the top of the mountain
They sit still.

————

[*The hunter:*]
Over there, far off, he runs
With his white forefeet
Through the brush.

Over there, near by, he runs,
With his nostrils open,
Over the bare ground.

The white tail, climbing,
Seems like a streak on the rocks.
The black tail, striding,
Seems like a crack in the rocks.

[*The deer:*]
Here I come forth.
On the earth I fell over:
The snapping bow made me dizzy.

Here I come forth.
On the mountain I slipped:
The humming arrow made me
     dizzy.

———

[*The hunter:*]
The black crows flying,
Having seen the snapping bow,
Toward it in a narrow line
Go flying.

The yellow coyote running,
Having seen the humming arrow,
Toward it crouching
Goes running.

———

[*A hunter, laughing:*]
I, very eager,
Grabbed the deer's foreleg,
Thinking it my bow.

I, over-brave,
Grabbed the deer's tail,
Thinking it my feathered arrow.

[*The deer:*]
Lo, surely I shall die.
Over there toward the west,
Here and there I went running.
Over there toward the west
There was a thundering;
It shook me.

Lo, surely I shall die.
Over there toward the east,
Here and there I went running.
Over there toward the east
There was an echoing;
It threw me down.

———

[*The hunter:*]
An old male deer is walking,
An old male deer is walking.
"An arrow is sticking in me,
There it is sticking.
My tail I shake,
My head I jerk."

An old male deer is running,
An old male deer is running.
"An arrow is sticking in me,
There it is sticking.
My tail I shake,
My head I jerk."

[*The deer:*]
You killed me.
I fell.
I knew not what I was doing
As I ran.

————

[*The hunter:*]
I am whistling.
Lo, I have found the deer!
I am whistling.

I am running and shouting.
Lo, I have killed the deer!
I am running and shouting.

————

[*The people:*]
Who is the man
Who has killed the old male deer?
Yonder he carries it on his head.
It is Wind Man,
Killer of the old male deer.
Yonder he carries it on his head.

THE PEACEFUL GO TO WAR

MOUNTING THE ARBOR beside his brush hut, the crier shouts into the glaring quiet of afternoon: "Come together! A man who was hunting has seen a thing to tell about. Come together!" Out in the fields men drop the slabs of wood with which they cut the weeds away from the corn; they seize the bows and arrows always lying beside them, and cluster around the council house. "To the east a hunter has seen Apache tracks. Let no one go far from the houses. Call home the women who are gathering roots. Tonight come to the council house. We shall talk of war."

The peaceful people do not go to war for glory. To them the hard journey over the mountains into the Apache country is a thing of weariness, even of horror. Not one word do their songs speak about magnificence of battle. But they must battle. In the mountains that bound their desert in crescent shape to the east and south is a tribe that does not sow nor reap. Its people are hunters and they have migrated, in that blind ebb and flow which received its impetus before written history began, to a land where the hunting is not good. The Apaches kill what deer and gather what seeds they can. But they have not the Papagos' painstaking lore of desert planting. Their only implement is the bow and arrow; and now they are hungry.

They wait until the peaceful people have garnered their spotted beans and their little hard corn. Then they swoop down from the hills. "You never knew, when you came out of your house in the morning, but an Apache might jump yelling off the roof."

Once the village of Mesquite Root was wiped out, the men killed and the women taken prisoner. Every village knows that this fate may some day befall it. But there is no wild rushing out with bows and arrows. This is an ever present menace and the people soberly plan to get the harvest in, if they can, before they go to war.

That night, they gather in the council house: rather, the men do; for the women never go there except to do the cleaning. It is the same squat dome of brush and earth which serves for fermenting the liquor and for all other village ceremonies. In its center a fire has been made by the nearest approach to an executive the village has, the Keeper of the Smoke.

He is an old man with many rituals in his memory, learned from some man in his family who was the Keeper before him. It is his duty to make the fire and tell the people what is forward. They have no other chief. The little company of kinsmen talks, smokes, talks, smokes, talks around the fire until all minds are at one.

The Keeper of the Smoke sits at the back of the council house, with the crier beside him. He sits cross-legged, his arms folded and his head on his breast, the ceremonial position. He does not move as the men come in in silence and take each his accustomed place. When all have come, he speaks.

"The tracks of two enemies have been seen, to the east of the village. They were going toward the hills and they have no horses. I think it well that a party of men should follow them, since we have men at leisure now. It is not the deer season and most have finished harvesting."

He speaks in a low voice and does not raise his head.

Why should he be excited? The men know how things are. They will go if they can. No one answers; for, before minds are made up, the ceremonial cigarette must go round. That name, with its sophisticated connotations, seems unsuited to this original cigarette, a length of hollow reed stuffed with wild tobacco. The Keeper puffs it four times, then hands it to the man at his right.

"My younger brother!"

"My elder brother!"

This is the most usual salutation, for cousins of all degrees are brothers in the Papago system of kin. Papago has no small words of courtesy, and all our ideas of greeting, respect, and affection are summed up in the use of the term of relationship. It means loyalty, it means mutual memories, mutual possessions, mutual obligations.

All round the circle goes the cigarette, one man smoking at a time. Softly another old man speaks: "I think it well." Farther down the line another murmurs: "I think it wiser to wait. Two days ago a boy reported tracks to the west. There may be another party." Another says: "Let us ask the neighbor villages. It is time to punish them well."

There is no voting at this meeting. The cigarette goes round and there are long intervals of thought until the men have compromised and reconsidered and at last agreed. It is the old men who speak: the young ones, who will do the fighting, are sitting in the background. They have been taught, from earliest childhood, not to interrupt, not even to add their word in the presence of the old men, unless they have important information. There are no castes in this society except the castes of young inferiors and old superiors. The turn of the young men comes at the end of the night, perhaps at the end of three

or four nights, when the policy is decided. Then the
Keeper of the Smoke inquires, still in his low, ceremoni-
ous tones, as he glances about the circle:

> "What men wish to go to war?"

He makes no other appeal. He does not need to. The
men have been trained from babyhood in the solemn ad-
jurations of the war poetry:

> "Thus should you also think and desire,
>   All you my kinsmen."

They know that a man who does not do his duty will
fail to share in the unity of the kin. No rebuke will be addressed to him. His neighbors will give him deermeat and
corn when they have it, just as he gives to them. But there
will be a gathering together of the others from which he is
excluded, just as a child is excluded from the harmony of
its elders. In a circle of twenty men this exclusion is a
harrowing thing. Some men escape it only by putting on
women's dress and grinding corn and gathering seeds with
the women.

One by one the young men speak in a low voice, volun-
teering. There are some who may not go because their
wives are with child. They chafe at the restriction put
upon them, but they dare not disobey it. To try to kill at
such a time would be an unholy act and the killer's hand
would lose its strength. He must not raise it, even against
a deer or a rabbit, and if he should venture to confront
the enemy he would be killed himself or he would come
home to find the child dead. At home, the pregnant
women who know that they, at least, will not be widowed
this time, are filled with guilt or elation according to their
characters. Did one of them, one wonders, ever dare to

feign pregnancy in order to keep a young bridegroom by her side?

When the young men have volunteered, they leave the council house. It is not for them to make the plan of war or to choose the leader. The old men do that and the young men may sleep. It may be they will be waked before dawn and told to be on their way toward the enemy's mountains. But it may be that the danger is over. The old men send out a runner; the tracks point back toward the Apache country; there is time to get the harvest in. But when the crops are garnered and hidden in buried pits; when the intervillage games are over; when the last drop of water is dried out of the valley and everyone must move to the mountain springs, then comes the yearly time for war. The peaceful people undertake it with the sober determination with which they go for days without water or live for a month on roots and stalks when the food is exhausted. But, once a year, they feel it their duty to put fear into the enemy.

It is not a war of the Papago nation, for there is no nation. Each village has a few neighbors whom it calls kin and upon whom, out of all the villages of the Desert People, it relies as comrades. Three or four comrades provide a force of twenty men. That is the punitive expedition. The council sends to each of the comrades a youth carrying a stick with ten notches. That means that on the eleventh night the warriors will meet at the foot of the enemy's hills. No comrade refuses. The law of helping one's kin is the fundamental law of Papago life: one could not deny it and continue to live among his own people. But no one, even in the village which initiated the expedition, pretends that he desires it.

Every night the warriors gather in the council house

and every night the ritual speaker, who knows the war poems, recites them in a low voice as a spell for power. They are, like other war poems, a means to work men up to the ordeal which is before them. But they do not mention war. Men are urged to do their duty in response to a call that cannot be denied, the call of kin. But the reward which is offered them is not glory. Personal glory is, indeed, a conception unknown to the Papagos. Nor is it revenge. The poems sometimes do not mention the enemy and certainly they do not mention death. They speak of the one end and aim of Papago life: rain. This means to life in the desert seems always like a miracle which may never be beheld again. So basic is the necessity for it, so profound the longing, that the imagination conceives of no other good thing. Glory is for people less concerned with dire necessity. To the Papago, his sacrifice and daring would be futile if it did not bring the one desired boon: rain and the growth of seeds.

The war orator, with head bowed, speaks in a low voice. His words are a spell rather than a plea to human ears:

> Is it for me to eat what food I have
> And all day sit idle?
> Is it for me to drink the sweet water poured out
> And all day sit idle?
> Is it for me to gaze upon my wife
> And all day sit idle?
> Is it for me to hold my child in my arms
> And all day sit idle?
>
> My desire was uncontrollable.
> It was the dizziness [of battle];
> I ground it to powder and therewith I painted my
>   face.

It was the drunkenness [of battle];
I ground it to powder and therewith I tied my hair
    in a war knot.
Then did I hold firm my well-covering shield and my
    hard-striking club.
Then did I hold firm my well-strung bow and my
    smooth, straight-flying arrows.
To me did I draw my far-striding sandals, and fast
    I tied them.

Over the flat land did I then go striding,
Over the embedded stones did I then go stumbling,
Under the trees in the ditches did I go stooping,
Through the trees on the high ground did I go
    hurtling,
Through the mountain gullies did I go brushing
    quickly.

In four halts did I reach the shining white eagle, my
    guardian,
And I asked power.
Then favorable to me he felt
And did bring forth his shining white stone.
Our enemy's mountains he made white as with
    moonlight
And brought them close,
And across them I went striding.

In four halts did I reach the blue hawk, my guardian,
And I asked power.
Then favorable to me he felt
And did bring forth his blue stone.
Our enemy waters he made white as with moonlight.
And around them I went striding.

There did I seize and pull up and make into a
    bundle
Those things which were my enemy's,
All kinds of seeds and beautiful clouds and beautiful
    winds.
Then came forth a thick stalk and a thick tassel,
And the undying seed did ripen.

This I did on behalf of my people.
Thus should you also think and desire,
All you my kinsmen.

The men listen until the morning star appears and
then go back to their work of preparation. Each one provides his own armament, and some otherwise brave men
must stay at home because they cannot manage it. This
does not imply shiftlessness, for Papago preparedness in-
volves the foresight of a year or more.

There are first the war arrows. These are not like deer
arrows tipped with light stone, or rabbit arrows made of
wood only. They are tipped with heavy quartz found only
in four places, and having magic powers because it is the
congealed blood from a hero's wounds. A man must have
made a long journey to get it, and must have flaked it with
a deer antler, over months of labor. He must have gathered reeds for the shafts in the season when reeds were
fresh. He must have hard wood for the foreshafts, sinew
and gum for the binding, and eagle tail for the feathers;
also an old man who knows the arrow songs. If he has shot
off all his arrows on a recent war party and since then has
been tilling the ground for his kin, there is no hope. No
one will give him war arrows: their possessors have too
dire a need of them.

The Papago in war: war leader reciting ritual; war headdresses; war paint

Of course, his bow is ready: he would no more leave the village without it than a modern man would journey without money. But he needs two new bowstrings. If he is supervaliant, he carries a club and a shield wherewith to finish off the enemy at close quarters. The clubber, who goes into battle ahead of the bowmen, is always prepared.

His ironwood club, shaped exactly like a murderous, sharp-edged potato masher, needs no renewing, and the round buckskin shield has nothing to get out of order but the deer-hide grip across the inside.

A man's costume in civil life is a breechclout only. For war, he adds sandals and a headdress. There must be two pairs of sandals, one pair to wear through the thorny wilderness and one pair to carry. He may have to make them both new, even to the killing of the mountain sheep. But if all this arduous labor is done, he may have time for the glamorous part of his costume, the headdress. Papagos did not wear the kingly war bonnets of the Plains, which ridged a man's back with eagle feathers; they wrapped their long black hair in a bun at the back and tied it with a headband of undyed, hand-woven cotton. The ordinary warrior painted the parting of his hair red, and that was all. But he who wished to express his personality made a skull cap of buckskin and fastened to it a flopping topknot of hawk or eagle feathers.

> Feather Mountain stands far away.
> Thither I crept [through the underbrush
>   to spy on the enemy]
> With my feather headdress shaking.

The ten days are up. On the eleventh the men start with the rise of the morning star, the beginning of the Papago workday. It is cold and going to be colder in the mountains, but they wear no clothing: in fact, they have none; they supply its place with grease. Over the grease they paint their faces with red and black, and all draw black lines under the eyes to make them keen. Black paint is the visible sign of the madness of war. Each one carries an extra pouch of it to blacken his whole face in the event he should become that contact point of dangerous magic, an Enemy-slayer. Their belts are strung with equipment like a rack of implements. The club hangs at the back like a workman's hammer. The quiver is at the left side. At the right are the extra sandals, the tobacco pouch, the paint pouch, the drinking gourd, and the sack of parched corn meal. The little sack of meal constitutes the only ration for this army; unlike Napoleon's, it does not travel on its stomach; it travels on magic.

MEETING THE OWL

THE PARTY of twenty or thirty men has arrived at the borders of Apache country. After this, they will sleep by day and travel by night, making no sound and going almost without food and water. Tonight, the detachments from the different villages have met, and they sit in a circle with its opening toward the enemy.

Each man has at his belt a pouch of parched, ground corn meal, a clay water pot in a grass bag, and half a gourd. These constitute his camp kit. He pours into the gourd a little corn meal and then a little water, stirs it with his finger, and drinks. This is the famous *pinole*, food and drink in one; already cooked, so that no fire is necessary. It is the only ration of the Papagos for war and hunting. Even now, I might add, when an old man is sick and needs to have his palate tempted, he will refuse hospital delicacies and beg for *pinole*.

Tonight, there will be no sleep; for it is the night to make magic so that the enemy will be blind and helpless. This is the night to call on the supernatural powers for help, the night for the medicine men to talk with the dead and discover the enemy. Through the darkness the herald can be heard calling the magicians to the circle: "Medicine man! Owl-meeter! My kinsman! You must be somewhere. Come forward."

Silently, the medicine men rise from the groups of their fellow villagers. Their faces are blackened to make them "see" better. They carry with them the shining stones which are to throw light on the path of the enemy. Perhaps they have tobacco to offer to the supernatural beings who must advise them, for these medicine men are chosen because they are "Owl-meeters." Owls are the bodies taken by dead Papagos when they wish to visit their home country, and a man who can meet the owl and talk with him can get news from almost anywhere, especially if he can call an owl who was once a Papago warrior killed in the Apache country and familiar with all its happenings. The intrepid medicine men must call such owls and must see just where the enemy can be ambushed, or they lose their standing. But they get no compensation. "This is for the whole village and they are part of the village." It is their duty.

The medicine men take their places inside the circle, with their faces toward the distant enemy. At the right of the last man is a spear, stuck into the ground. The spear is an Apache weapon, not Papago, but this one is to be grasped and held by each speaker as he concentrates the purpose of the men on war.

Directly behind the medicine men sits the war leader, with his face also toward the enemy, and on his right sits the herald. There is no wild cheering, no dance. The leader speaks with bowed head and in a low voice. He is not inciting the men. He is pronouncing a charm which will make victory sure for his side—or, if not victory, then a sense of duty done. The charm is only the tale of a legendary successful war party in past days, but this telling of past happenings, in ritual words, with danger ahead, is powerful magic. One of the two who knew it refused to recite it to me because to repeat it purposelessly might cause his death.

SPEECH AT THE FIELD RENDEZVOUS

(Santa Rosa)

Thus did I do:
All the sticks which I had broken did I knock
    down
One after another.

Then did my relatives come from all about
    and stay here ready.
My poor food did they eat and stay here ready.
My water did they drink and stay here ready.
The sun went down.
Then did I take my burning firebrand and
    yonder a little way go carrying it.

Yonder a little way off on the sand I placed it,
That we might have a night of ceremonies.
There did I sit, and soon they came to me, my
    young men.
With them all night I held the ceremonies,
And soon it was morning.

The next night again I took my burning fire-
    brand and yonder on the same camp-
    ground I placed it.
Soon from all directions came my young men.
With their help did I kill many big-eared hares
And many winged flying things.
Further in a river-bed we camped.
It was a night of ceremonies.
Around us the yellow fat of our kill turned
    to ashes.
We ate the food half cooked, longing for dawn.

From Sleeping Eagle came the youth and
        told me,
"Some game that they have killed I found there
        lying," he said.
"Good. Lie still and look.
Continue spying out that we may know their
        doings."
Thus I said.
And I sat warming myself by a small fire.

From Water Source came the youth and
        told me,
"Some game that they have killed I found
        there lying," he said.
"Good. Lie still and look.
Continue spying out that we may know their
        doings."
Thus I said.
And I sat warming myself by a small fire.

Again I said:
"What has happened?" [The scout answered:]
"The outspread earth lies quiet,
The embedded rocks are quiet,
The standing trees are quiet,
The running creatures run quietly."

Again I said:
"What has happened?" [The scout answered:]
"The outspread earth lies quiet,
The embedded rocks lie quiet,
The standing trees stand quiet,
The running creatures run quietly."

Then thus I said:
"Come now. Get ready, my young men."
Then I stood and made the war speech.

THE FIGHT

Then one of my youths
Made himself like a gray snake
And went crawling round a rock on hands
       and knees
Behind. Then one of my youths
Made himself like the killer wildcat
And went crawling along a ditch on hands
       and knees.

Morning began to run upon us.
Then, leaping, in we went.
Out came a lone enemy, and, looking about
       in surprise,
He broke a tree and down went rolling.
Then Rattlesnake, who kills with his mouth,
Took his body and went dragging it along.

Out came another lone enemy.
Looking about in surprise, he slipped on the
       grass and down he went rolling.
Then Hawk, who kills with his claws,
Took his body and went dragging it along.

Then did the sun reach the rising point.
Then no more did we wrestle.
We made an end of them.

Thus, perhaps, do you also think and desire,
All you my kinsmen.

After the war speech comes the singing, which is magic made by all the fighters together. They sing the enemy blind and deaf; they sing power upon themselves.

WAR SONGS

Gray owl medicine man,
Come with me!
Yonder find my enemy
And make him helpless!

———

Blue hummingbird medicine man,
Come with me!
Yonder find my enemy
And make him helpless!

———

The wind keeps running with me.
With it, I run far yonder.
My enemy dizzily staggers forward.

———

The clouds keep running with me.
With them, I run far yonder.
My enemy drunkenly staggers sidewise.

———

Here I come forth!
With the wind I come forth
And come hither.
This, my cigarette smoke,
I blow against the enemy.

Here I come forth!
With the clouds I come forth
And come hither.
This, my cigarette smoke,
I blow against the enemy.

Gopher medicine man,
Gnaw the bow
Of this my enemy.

Hoot owl medicine man,
Cut the arrow feathers
Of this my enemy.

———

Very angry
To the flat land he came,
My enemy,
Exceedingly angry.

Very angry
To the mountains he came,
My enemy,
Exceedingly angry.

———

The bitter wind I cause to blow.
Therewith my enemy drunkenly
Staggers forward.

The bitter wind I cause to blow.
Therewith my enemy dizzily
Staggers sidewise.

———

[*The Papago:*]

My crooked club
At the west came forth.

[*The enemy:*]

There, even the enemy maidens
Seeing, laughed at me.

[*The Papago:*]

My flat shield
At the east came forth.

[*The enemy:*]

Then, even the enemy children
Seeing, laughed at me.

Coyote, our comrade,
We meet the enemy!
Tomorrow, fight!

At the last song, one of the fierce shield-and-club men
dances in the trail with his face toward the enemy, leaping
furiously in the darkness. With the last words he crashes
the club on the shield and every man in the circle pounds
his bow on the ground while he gives a war whoop.

Then there is silence. The leader calls to the medicine
men who have sat quietly in the dark, not singing:

"Medicine man, my kinsman, have you anything to
tell us?"

They tell of one medicine man who replied, "I think
I shall have something." He rose and went away in the
dark and they could hear him giving the call of an owl.
Then came his voice, talking to someone, but they heard
no answering words. "I will see," said the medicine man,
and he returned to the circle. "Has anyone some of the old
tobacco, the kind we used to raise?" One warrior silently
handed some to him, and the medicine man went back.
They saw him light two cigarettes and saw one passed
out into the darkness where no shape was visible. Both
cigarettes glowed intermittently as they do when being
smoked. The medicine man returned. "It is a dead Papago

warrior. He will fly over the Apache country and bring us news before morning." Before dawn, the medicine man reported: "At that gap which you can see beyond the palo verde trees, the enemy will be passing at noon tomorrow. We shall kill them all." And thus did it come to pass. But had it not, the medicine man might have been killed.

THE SCALP DANCE

WITH THE DAWN the raiding party rushes on the camp of the enemy. If all the men are absent from it and those to be killed only women, that makes no difference. Papago warfare comes too near to dire necessity for any chivalry. All the enemy are magicians. Their terrific power in battle shows that, as do also their strange garments, their weapons, their familiarity with the unknown mountains. If one of these magicians, male or female, is killed, the enemy power is by so much lessened and the killer is a hero.

But heroism of this sort is like taking the vows of some powerful secret order. The hero has put himself in touch with supernatural power. He must now put forth his utmost efforts to withstand its impact lest he too be destroyed. His hand, which has touched magic, might fail to strike; his bow might not shoot and his shield might become as a cobweb. He blackens his face in sign of what has happened and stands apart. Soon others join him and the war leader may find that half his little band are out of active service. But that indicates that three or four scalps have been taken, and it is enough. The punitive expedition starts for home.

The war party takes no booty and no captives, for these are not people who wish to glory over the enemy. War to them is the serious and painful business of a struggle against evil magicians. If they can frighten them off for a little while, it is well. If they can gain some of that magical power by dangerous ceremonies, they will venture it,

for the common good. But let none of the strange possessions of the enemy, in goods or in women, be brought to
camp. Who knows what evil might emanate from them!

The raiding party starts for home, but it leaves the
killers behind. The lot of those heroes will be the opposite from what it would be in our society, where glory
means public recognition. In fact, from now on, as important men, they will shun publicity, but their penance
must be described, as it occurs, later, after the triumphant
return of the nonkillers.

> They have returned upon their trail.
>
> They looked about them.
> All kinds of butterflies and birds
> They saw beside the road.
>
> As they were going,
> From above a whirlwind followed them,
> Madly twisting.
> It was the thing which they desired
>   to see.
> For this they came.

Thus a subsequent war speech describes the return of
the victorious party. Instead of booty, they bring with
them the whirlwind that means rain, and the birds and
butterflies that come with moisture.

The party shows dramatic instinct, for, no matter when
they sight their native village, they always camp outside
it for the night so that they may make a triumphant entry
at dawn. Long before dawn, they send out the fastest runner, who pauses within shouting distance of the village to
yell the names of the heroes.

> Yonder a man runs shouting, saying,
> "Seclude my wife";
>   The Enemy-slayer saying,
> "Here, long since, has my shield been painted."

Thus runs a scalp song. But generally it is the messenger who shouts the names of the men who have been secluded, lest their power harm others. And this means that their wives must be secluded, also. Meekly the wives leave their homes and go into retreat, before the victorious party arrives.

If a hero has daughters, they stay in the house, out of sight. But the girls who do not come within the scope of enemy power rush out to meet the heroes and escort them, singing, to the village. In their midst is one of the enemy scalps, mounted on a pole so that no one need touch it. The sight of the scalp evokes the wildest songs in the Papago repertory. They carry it to the village and hand it over to an old woman. She is one whose hereditary right it is to hold the scalp pole and to dance with it, for solo dancing, among the Papagos, is the special privilege of old women. "Young women would feel shy," but the old, instead of being pushed to the rear ranks, are expected to do the wildest dancing.

> Here I stand
> And sing for the scalp.
> Come and see, O women!

With this song the fearless crone carries the dreadful thing through the village and to the dance place in front of the council house. It is here that the pole is set up to be gloated over for sixteen days, while the killers are being purified.

The old woman dances with the scalp

Elder Brother taught the people this custom. When he himself was killed, it was Buzzard who, at the people's request, succeeded in despatching him, after a duel of magic. So, Elder Brother, when he came from the under-world with his conquering army, sought revenge on Buzzard. He captured him, and Buzzard begged for his life: "Do not kill me. Only take my scalp. I promise you that I myself will dance and sing around it. I will sing you the songs that make scalp magic." So, Elder Brother scalped Buzzard and he now has a bald head. The people hung his scalp on a pole and he led them, singing.

> Hey, hey!
> In a circle jump and sing;
> Here we sing,
> Jump and sing.

Look up here!
Look up here!
Look up here!

Great doings with the scalp!
Great doings with the scalp!
The little Prisoner!
Hang it up, hang it up, hang it up!

Hey, hey!
We pull out your pin feathers!
We cut your throat!

Holding hands in a row we go,
Backward jumping,
Backward jumping;
Holding hands in a row we go.

Hey, hey!
Poor thing,
All sing.
All sing,
Poor thing!
Hey, hey!

So far goes the triumph, but there is no crescendo to
frenzy. On the contrary; next comes a verse in which the
old men pity Buzzard.

Hey, hey!
The old men are crying.

Elder Brother himself steps in. The leader of his people
notices that the babies, carried by their dancing mothers,

are crying with weariness. He devotes two songs of this dance of triumph to showing the mothers how to put their babies to sleep.

> Hey, hey!
> The children are crying,
> The children are crying.
> Here we sit down.
>
> Hey, hey!
> I put my nipple in your mouth
> And pat you soothingly.
> I put my nipple in your mouth
> And pat you soothingly.

The old warrior who sang me this song showed me carefully how the baby must be laid on the ground and allowed to suck until the last minute as the mother gently withdrew. The songs go on jeering at Buzzard's wife.

> Hey, hey!
> Great doings!
> We have not killed your husband.
> He is staggering,
> Sort of staggering,
> Over there staggering.
>
> A cactus plant had a flower.
> The little thing died, the little
>   thing died,
> Chirping.

There is a note of cruelty in it, but the Papago does not sustain such notes.

> Hey, hey! [sing the thirsty singers]
> From the gourd I will drink.

They trample the dance ground until they have to sing:

> Hey, hey!
> In a swamp we sing.

And the last song trails off:

> Sleepy, sleepy, sleepy!

Thus does the Papago enjoy his triumph, with intervals of simple practicality. Every night for sixteen days the people assemble at sunset—old and young; men, women, and children—to sing around the scalp. No one touches it in the meantime: "it is too dangerous." They are content to let it hang there like a caged enemy until the sixteen days of purification have made it safe.

At the end of those days comes a great feast. The heroes will be released from their confinement; the neighbor villages will be invited, and, when it is over, everyone will gamble and bet to his heart's content. On that night a fire is built in the dance place and war dancers are invited from the neighboring villages. These need not be warriors. They are men who know how to dramatize war, leaping around the fire with shield and club. Each is followed by his women, leaping and posturing as he does. These dancers, who get all the glory of the victory celebration, also get the pay. The members of each hero's family beggar themselves to make gifts of buckskin, beads, and horses because the dancers have done honor to one of their members. A chorus sings as they dance:

> At the foot of the east
>   I got drunk,   .
> My younger brothers;
> The white wind met me
> And drove me mad.

Kill the Apache!
Kill the Apache!
Dry the skin!
Dry the skin!
Soften it!
Soften it!
I am happy with it!
Aaaah!
But there are still some
    Apaches left.

All this time, while their deeds are being celebrated,
the heroes sit at a distance from the fire, in the cold.

THE PENANCE OF HEROES

IN PAPAGO PHILOSOPHY, the hero is not a man to be fêted and publicly acclaimed. The possession of power is dangerous, and the man who has acquired it must fast and dream lest he be ruined by the strength of his own great deeds.

The greatest of these is taking an enemy's scalp—the act which saves the very life of the village, and the act to which all young men are urged. But a scalp is fraught with power. The enemies are magicians, and their scalps have the power of the dead owners. The man who possesses one controls that power, as though he had a slave to fight for him and defend him. But only if he handles his magic with circumspection! He must train himself for its use and through all his life go in fear that his dreadful weapon may turn against him.

Each man who goes to battle knows what awaits him if he becomes an Enemy-slayer. He will be like one inoculated with a terrible disease. He will not dare perform the simple human acts of eating his fill, touching fire, or scratching his body, for these are so intimately connected with life that they might strengthen the magic. So many other acts are also dangerous that the man will need another man to watch over him, almost like a nurse. Before he goes to war, each man chooses an ancient warrior who has been through a like experience and who will be his guardian; his "made-father" is the literal Papago. That man's wife will guard the hero's wife, for such is their intimate relation that she, too, is subject to the spell. All his relatives to the last known degree must go through some gesture of purification. This is not making enemy-killing easy.

The raiding party starts home, but the heroes steal in, a day's journey behind them, like men in quarantine. Already they need a guardian, and some veteran of the party volunteers to care for them. What he must enjoin upon them is a regimen of solitude and starvation, and with each new prescription he demands in solemn ritual:

> Verily, who desires this?
> Do not you desire it?
> Then learn to endure all
>   hardship.

The first duty of the temporary guardian is to knot up the long hair of his charge, for from now until the end of his purification the hero will not venture to touch his hair or his body with his polluted hands. Already the speaker of the ritual is giving the young man material for dreams.

The war hero

ON TYING THE ENEMY-SLAYER'S HAIR

Am not I, even I, your guardian?
And I recite the ritual.

It seems that at the east there lives a great yellow
    buzzard,
A great shaman.
Surely he is your guardian and, arriving from there,
He reveals something to you.

But now you were acknowledged [an Enemy-slayer];
You made your request to him and wept.
Then he picked you up, and far he threw you.
You fell, half dead; you awoke, you came to yourself.

To the west then did you turn and see,
There hanging, powerful birds,
In all directions their great wings flapping.
Between those wings you rushed out on the right-hand
    side.
Toward the ocean hang powerful birds,
In all directions their great wings flapping.
Between those wings you rushed out on the right-hand
    side.
Toward the east hang powerful birds,
In all directions their great wings flapping.
Between those wings you rushed out on the right-hand
    side.
Toward the north hang powerful birds,
In all directions their great wings flapping.
Between those wings you rushed out on the right-hand
    side.

It was a twisting wind.
With it I knotted your hair at the back of your neck,
Twisting it as the wind twists.
With the remainder I tied it, handling you roughly.

Verily, who desires this experience?
Is it not you who desire it?
Then you must still endure many hardships.

Next, the guardian gives the hero a scratching stick, so that his hands need never touch his body.

Verily, am not I your guardian?
And I recite the ritual.

To the west you turned and saw
Great wingless birds.
Surely they are your guardians.
Thence they come and reveal to you
    something.

Their sharp wing feathers they pulled out;
They bent them into an arch,
And toward the east they threw them.

Then came great darkness,
Glorious dizziness, glorious drunkenness.
Therewith gloriously I knot your hair
At the back of your neck,
And a sharp stick now I thrust into it.

These vague visions of magic buzzards and great wingless birds must be a boon to the unimaginative young warrior. In our own society it is such men who come off best in battle, whereas the poet may be destroyed. But the Papago warrior takes a scalp only as a prelude to dreaming. The young brave whose bent is for action may dread the empty period set aside for visions and clutch at every image his guardian suggests. Fasting helps his susceptibility.

He never touches either food or water unless they are brought to him by his guardian. The food, at the best, is only parched corn meal poured into a gourd and mixed with water. The right gesture for the hero is to let it settle until the mixture at the top is almost as thin as water. This he drinks, and throws the rest away. "That shows he is brave," say the Papagos, and this sort of fortitude gains their admiration even more than the swift act of killing. They need such fortitude daily in their hard lives.

The first cup of water, after a day's march when fasting, must mean almost delirious relief to the hero; and thus the guardian presents it.

> Within my bowl there lies
> Shining dizziness,
> Bubbling drunkenness.
>
> There are great whirlwinds
> Standing upside down above us.
> They lie within my bowl.
>
> A great bear heart,
> A great eagle heart,
> A great hawk heart,
> A great twisting wind—
> All these have gathered here
> And lie within my bowl.
>
> Now you will drink it.

The quarantined party arrives outside the village but dares not enter it. Long since, their names have been shouted out by a messenger, their elected guardians straining their ears at the house doors to hear. As soon as each old man knows that his chosen protégé is a killer, he sends his wife to fetch the hero's wife. The old woman leads the young one away from the houses and builds her a shelter of boughs. There she must sit for sixteen days, never looking at the sun nor touching fire, and eating only such gruel and water as the old woman brings her.

Now the old man goes to meet the hero. He leads him to some place out of sight of the village and seats him under a tree.

> There is a tree standing alone,
> Casting a cool shadow.
> Under it you will seat yourself.
> Your child must not come near and
>   look upon you.
> Your wife must not come near and
>   look upon you.
>
> Verily, who desires this?
> Do not you desire it?
> Then learn to endure hardship.

Four times four days the warrior sits. At morning and evening his guardian brings him a cup of gruel, and if he is brave he takes only a sip. Every four days his drinking cup is thrown away, taking some of the contamination with it, and a new one is brought him. Every four days his guardian bathes him by pouring a jar of cold water over him as he kneels. On the same day that the guardian's wife is bathing the hero's wife, their grandmother is bathing the children, and every relative, even to the remote degrees, is bathing also. It is no small ordeal in the chill of a winter morning before dawn. Nor is it easy to get the water, and the women of the hero's family may have to go many miles over the hills, running at their steady dog-trot, with clay jars in nets on their backs.

All this time the hero sits motionless, arms folded, head on breast, his weapons beside him. Now, if there is any poetry in him, it will come to the fore. As the days of solitary starvation go past, it will be strange indeed if the "great wingless birds" do not at some time call out to him; if some form of words does not shape itself in his mind which he can call his own magic song. Papago demands are very lenient concerning what constitutes a song. Just a slight variation from the song one's uncle sang will be enough. But the man must be convinced that the dream is his own, for from that it gets its power. And who shall say that the overwhelming desire to dream cannot produce dreams, just as, with other races, waking trances are produced. At least, I have never heard of a hero who did not dream. The songs which come to him are his magic tools, for the rest of his life, wherewith to purify other heroes and to cure the strange ailments that emanate from enemy scalps.

Meantime, the guardian keeps the scalp in which is concentrated all the power of the dead enemy. He orders a basket to be made for it, one of the special kind which is used only for sacred things. If he is skillful, he twists the hair into the shape of a little man and clothes it with buckskin and feathers, like an Apache. It lies waiting the day when the warrior shall be purified and fit to receive it.

This day is the seventeenth after the retreat began. At night a huge fire is made on the dance ground and the paid dancers with club and shield leap around it, followed by their women. But the heroes sit far from the campfire, with their weapons beside them and their wives behind them. No man must lean back during the whole night and no man must leave his position. Even his relatives do not speak to him; instead, they heap up goods to pay the dancers, who perhaps are not warriors at all. Publicity and pay are for unimportant men, and the hero shows his greatness by going without them.

At last the dancing is over and the ancient warriors of the village make ready to receive the new hero into their company. Two by two they approach him, and each sings of his own dreams which he had when he himself was undergoing purification.

The eagle shield	The hawk club
Lies yonder far;	Lies yonder, near;
A green rainbow	A rosy rainbow
Beside it lies.	Beside it lies.
A soft rumbling,	A soft rumbling,
like thunder,	like lightning,
Shakes the mountains.	Shakes the flat land.

Putting the sacred scalp in
the basket

Then each blows over the hero a cloud of sacred tobacco smoke and greets him as a relative.

"My younger brother's child."

"My older brother's child."

"My younger brother."

This means the reception of the exiled man into everyday life. The beloved titles of kin are always on Papago lips. They are the only words used as greeting, or as applause when a man has done well. People use them daily instead of names, because names are either too holy and powerful to be "worn out" by use or they are shifting nicknames.

When the guardian's turn comes, he recites the last of his rituals. Although it deals with victory, there is no word of war. The Papago prefers to think of his enemy as being annihilated by mad winds and mysterious charms. His realism is reserved for "this my land" and the joy of homecoming.

ON SMOKING OVER THE ENEMY-SLAYERS AFTER
THE VICTORY DANCE

Thus did I wreak ill on my enemy by many
    devices—
Did cause him, as he fought, to become
    like a ghost and to fall asleep.
Thus did I wreak ill on my enemy.

Thus did I wreak ill on my enemy:
Those of his kind with whom he went
    about and talked
I did cause him to hate,
Becoming like a ghost, falling asleep.

Thus did I wreak ill on my enemy:
The child whom he caressed I did cause
    him to hate;
The wife with whom he lay I did cause him
    to hate,
Becoming like a ghost, falling asleep.
Verily it was this that I desired.

From the east did I cause to come
A white charm of forgetfulness
And beside his accustomed haunts I set it.
From the north did I cause to come
A red charm of forgetfulness
And beside his accustomed haunts I set it.
From the west did I cause to come
A black charm of forgetfulness
And beside his accustomed haunts I set it
From the ocean did I cause to come
A painful charm of forgetfulness
And beside his accustomed haunts I set it.

Then thus I did:
Some of his belongings I took
And high above me did throw them.

From the east then white blasts rushed,
From the west then black blasts rushed,
From both sides rushing together they
    lashed one another.
Beneath the rain I went snatching:
I seized my women,
I seized my children [whom he had
    captured];
Nor was it hard to do.

Then hither I came to this my land.
I stood upon it and stood firm;
I sat upon it and sat still.

Thus perchance should all of you think
    and desire,
All you my kinsmen.

    The ordeal is almost over. As the signs of sunrise appear, the guardian brings the basket containing the enemy effigy. "Prisoner," this is called, and it is like a powerful spirit imprisoned for the use of its master. But that power has to be confirmed by holding it up to the sun, which will reanimate it. The guardian knows where the first ray of the rising sun will strike, and he holds the basket toward it so that the enemy's soul can enter the effigy waiting to receive it. When this is done, he presents the basket to the warrior. It will be child and friend and servant to him, ready to help in all his enterprises, ready to guard his house, if only he does not forget to give it food, tobacco, and eagle feathers. The guardian lays it on his knees and he receives it, saying, "My child." Then his wife, who has sat behind him during the whole night's ceremony, also cradles it. Then each of his children holds it, saying, "My younger brother." At last the warrior closes the basket, laying the gift of tobacco inside it. Now he has "scalp power."

EAGLE POWER

O<small>NCE, BY MAGIC,</small> a man was transformed into a giant eagle which flew down from the mountaintops and destroyed the people. Elder Brother scaled the peak and killed the eagle, and after that he decreed that eagle feathers should have magic. They have magic for all Southwest Indians, for different legendary reasons. The Papagos do not trouble about the origin of the eagle myth, which must be as old as the sight of the powerful bird, circling above the heads of struggling men; for them, "the eagle is like a man," and killing him gives power.

When a man has not managed to scalp an enemy but wants his chance to dream, he kills an eagle. Its feathers are his lifelong treasure, for, as an old man said to me, without being able to find further words to clarify his meaning: "Eagle feathers are a *great* thing."

The downy breast feathers are rain magic, so like the clouds that they can summon them. The tail feathers are the best possible for arrows, "since the eagle is so brave." The wing feathers—at least the outermost ones—have a name all their own; they are "divining plumes" for the medicine man, who could not work without them.

It is not "given" the Papagos to cage eagles. If they want the feathers, they must brave the supernatural dangers of killing the bird. Then come the fasting and the dreaming. It is only a four-day experience, but it is like scalp taking, a chance—or shall we say an excuse—for starvation. One would suppose the Papagos starved often enough, involuntarily. But I suspect it is for just that very reason that they teach their young men to starve with fortitude. They need that fortitude even more than they need wild bursts of valor, so they hold it up as the highest achievement and make valor only a steppingstone. Thus can human nature be trained.

A young man, at the beginning of his career, kills an eagle to help him dream out his future. He waits till summer, when the eagles are feeding their young, and marks out a nest. Before he goes out he chooses his guardian, who must be an ancient eagle-killer. A grandfather who could not serve his grandsons on this occasion would feel the humiliation of a modern grandfather who could not help them in the business world. The man of influence in this Papago economy is the "ripe" man, with scalp power, eagle power, and, if possible, ocean power too.

The youth shoots his eagle with bow and arrow and signals to his guardian from a distance. He dares not approach the house in his dangerous condition. The old man guides him to a tree which will be his four-day shelter and there directs his plucking of the eagle. The guardian will not touch the dangerous feathers; he points to them with a stick.

The killer stretches the eagle out on the ground and takes out the downy breast feathers. These he puts in a buckskin bag and lays beside him. They will be his one reward, besides his dreams; everything else will be given to the guardian and the singers who purify him. Next he plucks the two top feathers from the right wing and from the left. These are known as divining plumes, and without them no medicine man could do his work. They are the fee of the guardian. They must be laid in a cross, the tip of the right one pointing east and the left tip south. Then come all the other wing feathers, the tips pointing, in turn, to each point of the compass. They go to the purifying singers, and so do the tail feathers which are laid above them.

The killer seats himself for his vigil, with the feathers beside him. He must have a special charm to serve him in the future, as the scalp serves the enemy-slayer. The guardian makes this of eagle down tied to the top of a short stick with native cotton string. It is a simple implement, the feathers white, the stick untouched by painting or carving. It looks a crude enough relative of the prayer sticks of the Pueblo Indians, painted differently for each occasion and topped with the bright plumes of every bird they know. Even less does it seem like the gorgeous feather wands and streaming headdresses of the extinct peoples of Mexico. Yet, belief in the magic of feathers and their acceptability to the gods is an old one with the Indians. Perhaps it goes back to some such sense as the Papagos have that feathers are kin to the clouds.

Now the young man dreams. Though the eagle he has killed is "just like a man," he is not an enemy. He has not really died, but has been released to his original form and that form is human. Like a man, the eagle comes to the dreamer and sings to him. This is when a young man

The eagle sings to the dreamer

knows what his career will be. One man I knew dreamed of gambling, a respected specialty among the Papagos. The eagle showed him how to cut the sticks for dice and how to paint them. He always won. Another saw himself running, racing with a hawk. He became a runner.

Sometimes a young man is not satisfied with his first dreams. He waits till next year and kills another eagle, for no one could bear the magic weight of killing two in a summer. Perhaps in that year his ideas have changed and his unconscious purpose speaks to him in different dreams. This happened to a man of aggressive purpose who finally became a medicine man. He dreamed first of gambling. Next year, his dreams were uncertain but he persevered. The third year, the dreams were mysterious and promised more. The fourth year, they were the dreams of a medicine man.

When the four days are over, the old eagle-killers come to sing the new one into fellowship. They sit in a circle around a small fire and each as he sings holds in his hand the stick topped with eagle down. When he has sung, he brushes the killer with the feathers and wishes for him all the singer's own success in life.

The songs call the eagle "dear little bird" and "older brother," and each must have a companion song telling of the hawk, the younger brother. In these songs, more than in any others, the Papagos use their sense of contrast. Their poetic words go in pairs: "eagle" and "hawk," "white" and "black," "valley" and "mountain," "wing feathers" and "down feathers." All are, to them, magic words with an evocative power which calls for no further description. Placing them carefully, in two opposed verses, makes a pattern in which they delight.

A black-headed eagle
On a low rock
Flapped its wings.

A white-headed eagle
On a low rock
Descended.

————

Eagle bird!
When he alights
There is a sound of thunder.

Hawk bird!
When he perches
There is a flash of lightning.

————

An eagle is walking,
Toward me it is walking;
Its down feathers blow in the breeze.

A hawk is running,
Toward me it is running;
Its down feathers ruffle in the wind.

————

Eagle, my older brother,
Like a bow, in every direction,
Your long feathers are bent.

Hawk, my younger brother,
Like arrows, in every direction,
Your down feathers are let loose.

I was drunk,
The wind blew hard;
Across a flowerless place of many
      winds
It took me.

––––––––

The Mountain of Reeds
Stands up at the west.
There an eagle cries,
The flat land resounds.

The Narrow Mountain
Stands up at the east.
There a hawk cries,
The mountains echo.

––––––––

[*The eagle wails:*]
Did you not treat me ill?
My beautiful child you took.
I am anxious,
All night I scream.

[*The hawk wails:*]
Did you not treat me ill?
My beautiful brother you took.
I am anxious,
All day I cry.

OCEAN POWER

BESIDES KILLING AN EAGLE or an enemy, there is a third way for a man to get dream power. (The word "man" is to be taken literally, for none of these experiences are open to women.) This third way is to go on the arduous pilgrimage to fetch salt from the Gulf of California.

The Gulf is four days' journey from the Papago country, and for unknown generations the Indians have been going there to hew out some of the rocky brown substance from the shores where standing water has left it. The almost waterless journey traverses some of the most sinister country on the North American continent and the Papago name for the south is "the direction of suffering." But they have never shrunk from suffering. Instead, they have made it the cornerstone of their philosophy and the passport of dreams. The salt journey has seemed to them difficult enough and the sight of the ocean amazing enough to bring a man into contact with the supernatural.

They regard the whole ordeal as they regard war. It is an arduous duty undertaken for the sake of the kindred, and the reward is rain. The ocean, say the Papagos, their sympathetic magic marching for once with science, is the source of rain, which is brought by the ocean wind. But they go on to say that the wind will only blow if men have been to the ocean and given it gifts. And men must take back with them those white kernels which the "outspread water" deposits on its shores and which resemble corn. In all the rituals, in fact, the salt is called "corn."

Every village, in the old days, made the journey and

The sinister desert

each had its ritual. Now there are only a few, but each of these few has an old man who is the hereditary leader. Leader and priest, in the Papago sense, are one, for the old man's chief duty is to recite the rituals and direct the ceremonies which will make the men "safe." He knows a special language which they will use on the journey, a language of roundabout phrases which the Papagos call "soft words." It would be dangerous for them to mention in bald terms the sun, the coyote, the horses, the drinking gourds, even the firewood. They will be too near the heart of power to venture such familiarity, so they learn to speak of the "shining traveler," the "burning-eyed comrade," the "friend," the "round object," and "the things piled up."

Every young man who is old enough volunteers for the journey. Once he has done so, he must go in four successive years—until the magic has been tamed. All his equipment must be new, for he cannot risk the danger that it might have come in contact with a pregnant woman or a menstruant. He makes his two pairs of sandals, his net for carrying the salt (in recent days, his net saddlebags), his bridle, and his gourd water bottle.

> Thus was my desire [begins a fragment of
>   an old ritual].
> Then hastily I ate the food which my wife
>   had cooked.
> Hastily I took my child in my arms.
> "What is it?
> What has he learned that he is acting thus?"
> "The day has dawned when I must go."

The party sets out in single file, formerly on foot and now on horseback. But it has not occurred to anyone to take extra horses for carrying the salt. They load their riding horses and walk home. They ride in single file, with the leader ahead, and they do not step off the trail lest they injure the house of some animal and incur its anger. When they camp, they lie with their heads toward the sea, so that "its power can draw them on."

The salt pilgrims

Camping, like all other steps of the journey, is a ceremonial act. There are three water holes in all that desert
waste, where many a Spanish explorer has perished. Two
must be reached on the first two nights, but no one drinks
from them without permission. First they give the water a
gift of eagle down and ask its help. Then they water their
horses, fill their gourds, and sit in a circle. Each youth
has his little pouch of corn meal, which he does not touch.
The leader takes it from him, mixes the meal with a little
water in his gourd, and hands it to him. The "brave" man
drinks only the thin solution on top and pours the rest
away. The man who turns his back so the others cannot
see how much he drinks is scorned.

Now the leader takes his place in the center to recite
the charm which controls the supernatural force about
them and turns their hardship to power. Some phrases
of this charm echo those of an ancient Aztec prayer to
the rain gods. But the sonorous words of supplication
for the dry earth are prefaced by a Papago scene, and
from its realism one could almost draw the hut with its
thatch, its center post, and the dried ashes outside. In
these familiar surroundings a man has worked himself
up to the emotional tensity of desiring a vision. Many a
youth who knew that on a vision depended his career
must have felt this half-sane restlessness that ended in
frustration. The cure is tobacco smoke. Four puffs of it
bring the smoker into the supernatural world, face to face
with the rain god.

(Anegam)

Food she cooked for me,
I did not eat.
Water she poured for me,
I did not drink.
Then thus to me she said:
"What is it?
You did not eat the food which I have cooked;
The water which I fetched you did not drink."
Then thus I said:
"It is a thing I feel."

I rose and across the bare spaces did go walking,
Did peep through the openings in the scrub,
Looking about me, seeking something.
Thus I went on and on.
Where there was a tree that suited me,
Beneath it prone and solitary I lay,
My forehead upon my folded arms I lay.

There was an ancient woman.
Some lore she had somehow learned
And quietly she went about telling it.
To me she spoke, telling it.
Then did I raise myself upon my hands;
I put them to my face and wiped away the dust,
I put them to my hair and shook out rubbish.

I rose. I reached the shade before my house.
There did I try to sit: not like itself it seemed.
Then did I make myself small and squeeze through
    my narrow door.

On my bed I tried to lie: not like itself it seemed.
About me with my hand I felt,
About the withes that bound the walls I felt
Seeking my jointed reed [cigarette].

Then thus I did.
Within my hut I tried to feel about with my fingers.
At the base of my hut, in the dirt,
I tried to feel about with my fingers
Seeking my jointed reed.
I could not find it.
To the center of the house did I go crawling
    [the roof being low].
And the center post
Seemed a white prayer stick,
So like it was.
At its base did I go feeling in the dirt
Seeking my jointed reed.
I could not find it.

There did I seize my flat stick [for hoeing];
I leaned upon it.
I made myself small and squeezed out the door.
Lo, I saw my ashes in many piles.
Already were they all hardened and all cracked.
I sat down and with the hoe I went to breaking
    them.
Among them, somehow, did I find my reed joint.

Then did I scratch it.
Lo, there still tobacco lay.
There beside me then I saw
Near me, lying, a shaman ember charred.

Long ago had it grown moldy and full of holes.
I took it up and four times hard did shake it.
Within, a spark burst out and brightly burned.
Then the reed joint did I light and to my lips I
    put it,
And somehow tried to move toward my desire.

[The speaker begins "throwing words".]
In what direction shall I first breathe out?
To eastward did I breathe.
It was my reed smoke in white filaments stretching.
I followed it and I went on and on.
Four times I stopped, and then I reached
The rain house standing in the east.
Wonderful things were done there.

All kinds of white clouds thatch it.
All kinds of rainbows form the binding withes.
The winds upon its roof fourfold are tied.
Powerless was I there.
It was my reed smoke.
Therewith did I go untying them.
Quietly I peeped in.
Lo, there I saw
Him [the rain-maker], my guardian.
Yonder, far back in the house, facing away from
    me he sat.
My reed smoke toward him did circling go.
Toward the door it caused him to turn his eyes,
And set him there.

Then did I say:
"What will you do, my guardian?
Yonder see!
The earth which you have spread thus wretched
    seems.
The mountains which you placed erect now
    crumbling stand.
The trees you planted have no leaves,
The birds you threw into the air
Wretchedly flit therein and do not sing.
The beasts that run upon the earth
At the tree roots go digging holes
And make no sound.
The wretched people
See nothing fit to eat."
Thus did I say.

Then did the bowels within him crack with pity.
"Verily, nephew, for so I name you,
Do you enter my house and do you tell me
    something?
The people are afraid, none dares to enter;
But you have entered and have told me,
And something indeed I will cause you to see."

"But let me reach my house, then let it happen."

Then in his breast he put his hand and brought
    forth seed:
White seed, blue seed, red seed, smooth seed.
Then did I fold it tight and grasp it and rush forth.

I saw the land did sloping lie.
Before I had gone far, the wind did follow and
      breathe upon me.
Then down at the foot of the east there moved
      the clouds
And from their breasts the lightning did go roaring.
Though the earth seemed very wide,
Straight across it fell the rain
And stabbed the north with its needles.
Straight across it fell the rain
And stabbed the south with its needles.
The flood channels, lying side by side,
Seemed many,
But the water from all directions went filling
      them to the brim.
The ditches, lying side by side,
Seemed many,
But the water along them went bubbling.
The magicians on the near-by mountains
Went rushing out, gathering themselves together;
The storm went on and on.
It reached the foot of the west, it turned and
      faced about.
It saw the earth spongy with moisture.

Thus beautifully did my desire end.
Thus perchance will you also feel, my kinsmen.

The Papagos have worked out a peculiar form of de-
livery for this speech. The peoples who vary their music
by the use of different instruments have not explored the
possibilities of the human voice alone. But the Papagos,
whose instruments are the kitchen basket turned upside

down for a drum, or the drinking gourd sealed up with its seeds for a rattle, have utilized every change of tempo and of accent. While the speaker is approaching the vision, his sentences must be in a monotone moving toward the verb at the end, which is on a high note, tremendously accented. It is a style, like a tune, which is used for all introductions. But when the magic part of the speech is reached and the man is speaking to the god, he begins "throwing words." It is a panting, on one note, where each syllable stands out separate and accented, like the monotonous chugging of an engine. In all the "wise speeches," made on the salt journey, their magic part is pronounced in this way.

On the afternoon of the third day, they reach the third water hole, the last they will find. It is at the base of Mount Pinacate, famous in legend, from whose top they can see the ocean. The thirsty men do not touch the water until they have raced each other to the top of the mountain. There the desert people stand and look at "the outspread water." They stretch out their hands to gather in some of its power and they rub their bodies. Then they give to the mountain the eagle down they have brought:

> Lo, it is my own offering,
> Which I have carefully made and finished.
> I have come bringing it and thus I do:
> I offer it.
>
> See it and do for me increasingly.
> Grant powers to me:
> Great speed in running,
> Great industry,
> Great skill in hunting.

Grant powers to me:
Great lightness in running,
Great industry.

I will take them,
I will journey back
And I will attain my desire.
Not hard will it be to turn homeward,
Not hard to reach my land.

With the power from the ocean already upon them,
they go back for their last drink in twenty-four hours.
From here on, it is a race of endurance to get the salt and
to return. They ride that night as far as human beings
may, but they do not sleep until the leader has recited to
them the supernatural experience of the morrow. They
are to enter the "outspread water," they who perhaps have
never seen water more than three feet deep—never except
in rain streams which dry in a few hours. They are to step
into the appalling element and bring out a blessing.

SALT RITUAL IN CAMP—THE MARKING
(Anegam)

Thus was fulfilled my desire.

Toward the west a black road did lie.
Then upon it did I tread and follow it.
Four times did I camp and then did reach the
wide-spreading water.

Already had arrived the woolly comrade [Coyote];
Around us four times did he go circling;
And lo, already the white clay was mixed for me,
The owl feather for painting laid upon it.

To him did Coyote pull the young man and set
    him there.
With the clay across the heart he marked him.
Back he turned and on the right shoulder marked
    him.
In front he crossed and on the left shoulder
    marked him.
Back he turned and on the back he marked him.
Then well he purified him.

There was corn meal, made from flat-headed corn.
I sprinkled a handful and again a handful,
As I ran into the wide-spreading ocean.
Though dangerously toward me it crashed
I did not fear,
But I walked near and cast the sacred meal.

There followed another wave.
I did not fear.
I walked nearer and cast the sacred meal.
Though dangerously it roared, combing and falling,
I did not fear.
I cast the sacred meal.

There followed a fourth wave.
Dangerously it roared;
It foamed, it rolled over me, it broke behind me,
But firm I stood and sought what I might see.

Then did I come forth
And along the beach begin to run
And somewhere there did come upon
Coyote, our woolly comrade,
Our comrade with burning eyes.

Dangerously he turned upon me,
But I ran toward him and did not fear.
Nearer I came and cast the sacred meal.
Then did he run, did run and run
Till at last he only walked.
And I did follow. And did come upon him.
In a circle did I run and come behind him.
I did not fear, but cast the sacred meal.

Again he dashed away.
I followed and did overtake him.
Then wild he barked and, crouching, turned to bite.
I did not fear, but cast the sacred meal.
Then he stood still and said:
"Verily, nephew, you will take away
All my powers together,
And more and more a seer you will be
Of mysteries."

He took me then, he took me.
He made me stand
Beside the wide-spreading ocean.
Under the spray that rose like smoke, he took me.
Across on the other side he brought me out
To a pool of water, thick as cactus juice;
He set me before it.

"Ready, nephew!
Now, if you are brave
You will drink all and you will take away
All my powers together."

Then down I threw myself;
I drank and drank,
I drank it empty, then I scraped the dregs,
Folded them up, and carried them away.

Then next he took me
To a pool of water thick with greenish scum.
He set me before it.
"Ready, nephew!
Now, if you are brave
You will drink all and you will take away
All my powers together."
Then down I threw myself;
I drank and drank,
I drank it empty, then I scraped the dregs,
Folded them up tight, and carried them away.

Then next he took me
To a pool of yellow water
And set me before it.
"Ready, nephew!
Now, if you are brave
You will drink all and you will take away
My powers with the drink."
Then down I threw myself;
I drank and drank,
I drank it empty, then I scraped the dregs,
Folded them tight, and carried them away.

Then next he took me
To a pool of bloody water
And set me before it.

"Ready, nephew!
 Now, if you are brave
 You will drink all and you will take away
 My powers with the drink."
 Then down I threw myself;
 I drank and drank,
 I drank it empty, then I scraped the dregs,
 Folded them tight, and carried them away.

 Then he stood still and said:
"If you shall take away
 All my powers together,
 Then more and more a seer you shall be
 Of mysteries."

 Then he went taking me
 And reached a land
 Which lies before the sunset.
 There abides the bitter wind;
 Not slowly did we go.
 About the wind's house, dust lay scattered wildly.
 Not slowly did he go and bring me there.
 Then leaping up did I stretch out my hand,
 I grasped the wind and slowly bent him down,
 Till blood drops trickled from him.
 Then from that house I seized
 A leather shield and a short club,
 A well-strung bow and smooth, straight-flying
       arrow.
 These did I bind together,
 And did return whence I had come.

That water did I reach
Which was thick like cactus juice,
And there a magician sat.
Coyote made me stand before him, saying:
"What will you do for this, my nephew?
I have brought him here."
Then forth he brought his white magic power
And placed it in my heart.

Then did I reach
The pool of water thick with greenish scum.
There a magician sat.
Coyote made me stand before him, saying:
"What will you do for this, my nephew?
I have brought him here."
Then forth he brought his green magic power
And placed it in my heart.

Then did I reach
The pool of yellow water.
Therein a magician sat.
Coyote made me stand before him, saying:
"What will you do for this, my nephew?
I have brought him here."
Then forth he took his yellow magic power
And placed it in my heart.

Then did I reach
The pool of bloody water.
Therein a magician sat.
Coyote made me stand before him, saying:
"What will you do for this, my nephew?
I have brought him here."
Then forth he brought
His red magic power
And placed it in my heart.

Then back Coyote took me, whence we came
And reached the wide-spreading ocean.
Under the smokelike spray he carried me
Even to that place where I had run along the
        beach,
And there he left me.
Then down I fell, but rose, and toward the east
        came running.
There sat our leader, head upon his breast.
He had not slept.
Straight to him walking, into his hands I put
The power I had won, tight pressing it.
Then I saw emerge
The sun, the gift of God.
Then up I looked, I followed the road.
I camped four times and reached my land.

The powers I had won, beneath my bed I placed.
I lay upon them and lay down to sleep.
Then in a little time mysteriously there came to me
Beautiful drunken songs,
Beautiful songs for the circling dance,
Beautiful songs for the maiden's dance,
Wherewith the maiden I might cozen.
My songs the stay-at-home youths did learn and
        sing,
Scarce permitting me to be heard.

With my songs the evening spread echoing
And the early dawn emerged with a good sound.
The firm mountains stood echoing therewith
And the trees stood deep rooted.

Speeches like these, recited year after year by the old men, are the patterns for dreaming. The young man, exhausted with hunger and effort, awaits his vision with these pictures in his mind. He will see Coyote as surely as the monk of the Middle Ages saw the saint whom he had made his patron.

It is on the morning of the fourth day that the travelers reach the barren sands where the spring tides have left salty ponds. Even these have evaporated, leaving an expanse of saline crystals, "the ocean's corn." No matter how great their thirsty hurry, the men do not gather them immediately. The leader must plant in the salt field a stick topped with eagle down, speaking in friendly fashion: "We do not come to harm you; we come only to gather salt." Then the young men run four times around the salt bed, and at last they all fall to, to load the horses. They explain to the salt, as the Papago always does when helping himself to the fruits of the earth: "We take you because we need you. Be light now, do not weigh heavy, because we must carry you home to the women."

This is the practical part of the labor, but the magic part, which has brought the young men on this long journey, is still to come. When the salt is gathered, they walk into the sea, strewing corn meal as the ritual bade them, on the advancing waves.

To the desert people, this braving of the breakers has an element of horror. Old men, who made no great matter of death and starvation, have told me with pride how they walked in up to their necks. My statement, that I had swum gaily beyond the breakers in two oceans, was the height of unwisdom. They regarded it as a lie.

A man holds corn meal in his left hand and throws it on the waves with his right. If he has done any evil, or if

his wife is "dangerous," the sea will not take his offering. But if it is accepted, perhaps then and there he may
see a vision. A flight of white gulls may beckon him into
the ocean depths, where he will learn wonders, or perhaps a strange sea coyote will come walking on the water
and speak to him. But many wait for a further trial, and
when they emerge from the water, they run for miles on
the beach. Running is the well-known way for a youth to
prove his strength and manhood, and running beside the
waves is something like the vigil of the oldtime knight
beside his armor. This is the most strange and sacred act
of a Papago boy's life. Perhaps a cave in the rock opens,
and he is asked in to learn the secrets of healing from the
sea magician. Perhaps a flock of white cranes overhead
calls him into the sky to race with them, or on the shore
he sees a set of magic gambling sticks made from shells
cast up by the sea.

   The oration tells how the leader waits, lonely and tired,
beside the campfire, until the last of the runners has come
in. Then, long before dawn, the whole party starts back,
for it must make each of the water holes for a night's
camp. The neophytes are now in a sacred condition. They
must not walk with the rest of the party, lest the power
with which they have come in contact prove too strong
for the others. They walk behind and they practice the
ancient ceremonial taboo used by most Southwestern Indians: they do not touch their bodies with their hands.
Each has a slender stick given him by the leader with
which he may rub his dry, sun-bitten skin. They must
never look back toward the ocean, for then it might call
them. Some villages forbid them to speak at all. There
are tales of men who have fallen into a pit and, because
they must not cry out for help, were left behind to die.

But when they reach the home village, they make a triumphant entry. The old women help themselves to salt, and the boys swing slabs of wood on long strings to simulate the sound of rain. That night, everyone gathers in the council house. The neophytes sit to one side with the trophies they have brought from the seashore—white shells or scraps of seaweed, "ocean clouds," which will act as magic charms for the rest of their lives. In the center is the basket of "sea corn." Each pilgrim has contributed to it some of his precious load, for

> "This did I do on your behalf,
> All you my kinsmen."

But no one can receive it until it has been purified and blest, like its bearers. The leader recites again the sacred phrases. They are the old, beloved ones, but their combination seems, on this occasion, to be reduced to its beautiful essentials.

> It was mysteriously hidden.
> Wanting it, I could not find it.
> Behind my house post did I thrust my hand.
> I could not find it. . . .
> I went out the door. There my ashes were
>   piled high.
> [With a stick] hard I struck them
> And out I took it—my reed cigarette.
> Burned out, it seemed.
> I scratched, and at the end
> Charred blackness lay.
> Four times I struck it,
> And out a great spark shone.
> I lit it in the fire, I put it to my lips, I smoked.

Then at the east a wind arose, well knowing
    whither it should blow.
The standing trees it went shaking,
The rubbish at the foot of the trees it piled.
A shining cloud toward the sky upreared
And touched it with its head.
All kinds of clouds together rose
And with it they did go.
Although the earth seemed very wide,
To the very edge of it did they go.
Although the north seemed very far,
To the very edge of it did they go.
Although the south seemed more than far,
To the very edge of it did they go.
Pulling out their white breast feathers
    did they go.

Then on it the old men in a circle sat
And held their meeting.
Then they scattered seed and it came forth.
A thick root came forth;
A thick stalk then came forth;
A fair tassel came forth
And well it ripened.
Therewith were delightful the evenings,
Delightful the dawns.

Then came the songs describing the thick root, the
thick stalk, and the fair tassel. They are the same as the
songs which sing up the corn, but a few breaths of the
ocean wind sound among them:

Now I am ready to go.
The ocean wind from far off overtakes me.
It bends down the tassels of the corn.

The ocean water hurts my heart.
Beautiful clouds bring rain upon our fields.

———

The outspread water!
Running along it,
I seized the corn.

———

The outspread water!
Running along it,
I seized the squash.

A ceremonial singer

   The music is made with the Papagos' most solemn ceremonial instrument. They turn over the willow kitchen basket, so tightly woven that it can hold the liquid porridge. On that, as a sound box, the musician rests a stick of hard wood, cut into notches all along its length. Then he scrapes another stick along the notches. It is a sound which our modern ears associate with the Negro dance orchestra, but the Papago does not use it for dancing. "Scraping" is our only word for translating a term which stands for the music of growth and which comes from the same root as "wind" and "the flapping of wings."
   The singing lasts until the morning star appears, and

then the old men purify the neophytes and welcome them back into the ranks of ordinary men. This is always done by blowing tobacco smoke over the man whose holiness is to be ended. The old man who blows the smoke says, "Hail, my kinsman," and then wishes for the boy prowess in hunting or running or whatever his ancient mentor has achieved. The boys are now almost men, but they dare not enter into their new state without a period of solitude and fasting. Each goes home to camp outside his own house, like a hermit, to eat sparingly of corn-meal gruel, and for sixteen days to wait for further visions. But he may come forth a man with a destiny; or so it seems to the fathers of eligible girls, and they often wait on his parents during the young man's seclusion. For no matter which vision has been his, he will emerge a "ripe" man to take his place with the warriors and councilors. He has helped to bring rain.

DANGEROUS WOMAN

THE REGULAR ROUTES to dream power are not open to women, who do not kill enemies or eagles and who are never taken on the salt pilgrimage. The woman of imagination and energy sometimes manages, from a cold start, to dream enough to become a medicine woman, but this does not happen often.

Woman has, however, one direct contact with the supernatural denied to men. So mysterious do her female functions appear to the Papago that he places every woman, when under their magic influence, in the category of a man undergoing purification. No man would approach such a woman, any more than he would the scalper or the eagle-killer in his retreat. The awful power which fills her would disable him, destroy his weapons, and cripple his tools. Even a dish from which she had eaten would convey to him the contamination.

So he segregates her as he does the warrior, the salt pilgrim, and the eagle-killer. But her segregation is not for sixteen days which end in triumph. Once a month, the woman must leave her house and hide herself from the sun and fire. When her children are born, she must stay in retreat "until the moon comes back where it was" before she can be purified. She expects no dreams at this time, for she has performed no act of valor. Hers is a negative purification, ordained without her will and serving only to make her fit for human intercourse again.

In preparation for this part of their lives, the women of the family build themselves a hut away from the main house. They do not regard their ostracism as a burden. From infancy they have expected it, as white girls might expect school and work. "It is not good when it is cold," they say. Otherwise, those monthly four days of peace and

A Papago woman with her
carrying net

solitude are a sort of sabbath in their toilsome lives. So deeply do they feel their own dangerousness that they would not be happy in exposing their loved ones to it. There are Papago tales telling about lightning strokes which wiped out a whole family because one girl in it disobeyed the law. And a woman who visited a ceremony at this time would feel as guilty as a disease-carrier who distributed death among her unsuspecting kindred.

There are alleviations in this recurrent purification which the men do not have. The woman, who will have no visions, need not fast. She is not forbidden the society of other women who know the mystery. So, for the only times in her life, she is away from the baby and the housework. She can sit at the door of her hut and chat with her friends, and her husband may not even call to her. No matter what she has left undone, and no matter what there is to do, she has a holiday. The villagers tell of women who always found themselves "dangerous" when their husbands grew quarrelsome. It has compensations.

The time when a young girl enters upon this state, which links her to the supernatural, is a point of great sensitivity in her career. If she is lazy in these first days, she will be lazy ever after; if she talks too much, she will be garrulous; if she has lice, she will never be free from them. Her mother watches for the moment so that she may ward off these dangers with admonition and discipline. Her father watches for it because he, the head of the house, must see that she is properly purified. If he should fail to do it, lightning might strike the whole village. Fathers who erred in this way used sometimes to be whipped.

The segregation hut is ready, the girl is escorted to it, and an old female relative, the most virtuous to be found, goes with her. "Virtue," in this connection, is used in the Papago sense, which means industry and observance of ceremonial rules. In Papago life, a woman's virtue does not hinge on her marital relations, but on her diligence in feeding the family and keeping danger away.

The virtuous teacher starts the girl at making a basket and lectures her while she labors. "Be industrious. Fetch water, fetch wood. Get up early in the morning and start to work. Never stop working. Some day an old man will see you." (This is a modest circumlocution for "A young man will marry you." The girl must not think of that young man until he appears.) "When he does, feed him well. See that there is always fresh water for him to drink." (This admonition is not superfluous. Sometimes fresh water has to be carried ten miles or so from the nearest spring.) "When he wants to go hunting, do not cling to him; let him go. Even though he stays many days in the mountains, or anywhere else, let him go. If he does not hunt, there will be no food. Then the neighbors will feed you and you will be ashamed."

Each word of advice is murmured over a hundred times or so, but the Papago does not mind repetition. He likes to receive information by this half-conscious process, which is as though the words echoed and reëchoed in one's own mind.

The girl's retreat is for four days only, and on each one she must have a bath. "Girls who become maidens in the summertime don't know what hardship is," said an old woman to me. "To kneel naked out of doors before dawn while your mother pours cold water over your head—that is hardship. But it made me brave," she added contentedly, "and industrious. For my mother made the wish when she poured the water."

After the four days' seclusion, the girl is "danced" back into fellowship. She is danced by everyone in the village, with fullhearted abandon. Even though childbirth be fraught with mysterious influence, the Papagos rejoice that another woman has become capable of it, and it is perhaps the mixture of the sinister and the joyful which makes the maiden's dance the gayest time of the year.

Elder Brother himself was an expert singer at the maiden's dances—indeed, his too great abandon at these times was the reason for his killing. Every village has a

man or two who knows Elder Brother's songs and many
others who have dreamed the songs of fire and wind and
flowers which suit a maiden's dance. The singer's rattle
sounds at sunset summoning the people. He puts his arm
over the maiden's shoulders and they two form the center
of a line of men and women which dances back and forth
opposite another line whose center is the singer's wife.

"I used to get so tired," my old friend said to me, "I
would sleep while I was dancing. Then the singers
pinched my nose. Oh, that old man made me work so. I
used to run in the house and hide when the singing began."

"How many nights?"

"Until the moon came round again. Oh, I was thin, as if
I had been sick. And I had given away everything I had
to the people who danced with me, to pay them." She nod-
ded her head reminiscently. "Ah, those dances! There was
never any fun like them. The young men would travel
two or three days when they knew there was a maiden's
dance. Do you know the sound of the rattle when our people come up in the night to dance? Ah, *good!*"

> Poor little maiden!
> In the evening you will clasp hands.
> In the evening I arrive and hasten hither,
> Hither I hasten and sing.
> Songs follow one another in order.

> ———

> The shining mockingbird
> At evening could not sleep.
> When the moon was in mid-sky
> He ran to the maiden's dance.
> At early dawn
> High did he raise his song.

Crane birds!
At early morning
I saw them over yonder.
When day came, they descended,
Squawking.

———

On the flat land
A rain house stands
Covered with clouds.
Very white it stands.
Butterfly wings are about it.
I like it.
I saw it all.

———

Darkness reverberates.
It rolls me over and over.
Beside the singing place
I lie down.
Darkness reverberates.

———

I know not what I do.
Here I am lying.
Now I leap up.
Circling I sing.
I go about,
I leap up, circling I sing.
Circling I sing.

———

Come all! Stand up!
Just over there the dawn is coming.
Now I hear
Soft laughter.

MEDICINE MAN

A PERSON TO BE FEARED is the Papago medicine man. He gains his power by dreams, as other men do, but his dreams go farther into the unknown. He flies with eagles; he visits magicians beneath the sea; he hears songs which can bring rain and bring death. Great power passes through him, and it depends upon himself whether that power is used for evil or for good. The Papago is never sure which way the medicine man has chosen: he seems to cure, but, perhaps at a whim, he may begin to kill. Papago records are sprinkled with accounts of the lynching of medicine men. If a patient refused to get well, or a plague struck the village, it might suddenly occur to the people that their inexplicable misfortune came from the one man with great power. Then they surrounded him and clubbed him to death, and the council thanked them.

The man who chooses this dangerous profession must have brains. His reward is riches, and he is the only man in the village who really possesses any. Other villagers help each other and get in return only their food and the promise of help when they, in turn, shall need it. But the medicine man receives a buckskin or a string of beads, and even in these days he can demand a horse or a cow.

No one dares refuse him; no one, no matter what the provocation, dares make him an enemy. Only another medicine man, in fear of his own skin, will escape vengeance by saying, "It is not I who am causing death; it is my colleague in the next village." In this game a man needs a forceful character, for when medicine men accuse each other it is the least aggressive who goes down. So, among the Papagos it is the ambitious man and the individualist who dares to take a chance in medicine. That is the one place where he can express himself.

The medicine man has a peculiar place in the treatment of sickness: he is a diagnostician only. His work is to sing himself into a state of trance where he "sees the cause of disease." Then someone else must cure it. That someone else is a humble dreamer who receives no pay but his food, just like the men who help to build a house or to plant a cornfield. The medicine man, the consultant, is the only paid professional.

He arrives at night, the time when all singing is done. In a deerskin sack he carries his implements, four feathers from the tops of an eagle's wings and a rattle of hollowed gourd with a handful of gravel inside. In some secret place he carries his "shining stones," quartz crystals which light the way for him and glow like a torch upon lurking enemy or disease.

He sits cross-legged before the patient with the crystals before him and smokes a cigarette in silence and alone: smoking is not a convivial custom among the Papagos. Then begins the low, hoarse hum of his singing. There is a technique to medicine singing which no White can recognize until after many repetitions of the songs. At first no words are sung; there is only a hoarse humming of the tune, if we call tune the pounding insistence on one note with an excursion of two or three tones in each direction. Then comes the medicine man's special sound—the breathy croaking of the words which makes them incomprehensible. The doctor's songs are too precious to be learned by any bystander, and the house is, of course, full

of bystanders, for no Papago would ever refuse entrance
to his neighbors. At last the words of the song are sung,
and then there is humming and croaking again.

All the time, the rattle is moving in the doctor's right
hand. But do not think that the use of a rattle is without
its rules. When no words are being sung the rattle is
shaken horizontally. With the words there is a sharp ver-
tical stroke. The whiplike motion of his hard brown wrist
continues in one direction or the other all night.

After each song there is a pause. Then the eagle feathers, those very powerful plumes which must come from
the topmost feathers of each wing, and which also have
a technical name, are slowly waved over the patient,
"cleaning him." Or "some doctors jab them at the patient,"
I was informed; for bedside manners differ. Then the
doctor draws on his cigarette and blows the smoke all
over the patient, sometimes blowing some saliva with it.
That slowly wafting smoke will reconstitute a patient's
morale if the thing can be done. I have heard stories of
people who came back almost from the grave when they
smelled that "holy smoke." They believed.

The songs of the medicine man have nothing to do
with the patient. They tell of his own dreams. Some men
have strange ingenious experiences and some have comic
ones. It does not matter what the dream is, so long as it
takes the medicine man out of daily life into the realm
where power may be captured.

> Do you see, my younger brother?
> Now I sit down.
> My gourd rattle moves in a circle.
> Evening rushes out
> And yonder goes sifting down.

Do you see, my younger brother?
Now I sit down.
My gourd rattle moves in a circle.
Morning rushes out
And yonder goes shining.

———

At the shore of the river
The sun has just set.
I turn back; the mountain
Can no longer be seen.

———

A little gray horned toad
Came out of the darkness.
Right round he twisted,
Stretched out his neck
And spoke to me.

———

An earth crack,
An earth crack!
Out of it comes Elder Brother
And takes me to the sky.
Surely he will make me a medicine man.
What can you do to me!

———

A serpent hangs from the sky
With his head over the sea.
He is swaying his head to and fro
And singing.

DRIVING AWAY EVIL

THE INDIANS of the Southwest have a belief in witch-craft which even puzzles investigators, because it is so like our own traditions. But to them a witch is not purely evil. Rather, they think that power can be turned to either evil or good, and the same man can be a medicine man who cures or a witch who kills. So the medicine man is always regarded a little askance. He may, if he hates someone, plant an evil charm in that man's corn-field. The charm is an eagle quill stuffed with mysterious matter which he has taken from his heart. It sprouts as a seed sprouts, and finally bursts, scattering the evil through the earth and air. If it can be pulled out before it bursts, the charm is powerless; so it is the duty of a good medicine man to search out such charms, to see them by the light of his magic crystal, and to pull them up. Of course, this gives opportunity for the paying off of private grudges among medicine men, not to mention the alibi for one who cannot cure his patient. Such a man has only to say: "There must be an evil charm planted near the house. I will pull it up."

But he cannot go on his fearful errand alone, the whole village must sing to give him power. So the men gather in the council house and sing the songs to drive away evil. Then, with a few bold spirits in attendance, he goes prowling through the fields, drawn by his magic power toward the evil thing. Sometimes it glows like a light ahead of them; sometimes, frightened, it starts to burrow through the earth, and then he follows its trail above.

The cholla

Foul, foul [His helpers are singing.]
Here before me it is embedded,
It is moving to and fro.

When at last the medicine man has found it, he sends
his helpers to hide and, alone, he grasps the fearful thing
and pulls it out of the ground. No helper dares approach
until the medicine man falls fainting with a broken quill
in his hands. Many Papagos will testify to having revived
fainting medicine men and to having seen the quill or,
perhaps, merely a stick of wood which has once been an
evil charm, now powerless.

Sometimes an epidemic attacks the village and then the
evil cannot be confined in one spot. While the men sing,
the medicine man walks around all the houses with a
branch of cholla, the thorniest cactus known. This particular species is called by Whites the "jumping cholla,"
for they insist that its thorns actually jump out to clutch
the passer-by. Quite logically, therefore, the Papagos con-
sider that a branch of this cactus will catch and hold any
evil in the village. The medicine man carries it into every
corner, then takes it to the north, the direction of evil,
and burns it. The speech which was recited to me for this
occasion uses as a charm not the cholla, but the ocotillo,
whose whiplike branches, ten feet long, are set with

thorns as large and rigid as nails. It is spoken by a man who learned it from his father and, because it tells how disease was once conquered, it brings about another conquest.

SPEECH TO CLEANSE THE VILLAGE OF SICKNESS

Ready!
There did I call by the kinship term
The youth whom I had reared.
Toward the west was a black road made and
    finished.
Four stops made the youth and speedily did come
Where stood a black ocotillo.
Not slowly back to me he came and said:

"Within itself it rustles as it stands;
Within itself it thunders as it stands;
Within itself it roars as there it stands;
Within there is soft rain.
Around it four times did I circle
And toward the west a branch I broke with all
    my force.
I took it and to you I brought it."
Therewith a part of the sickness
Did I pound into the earth and stake it down.

There was toward the ocean
A road of many hardships made and finished.
Four stops made the youth and speedily did come
Where stood an ocotillo most painful to the touch.
Not slowly back to me he came and said:

"Within itself it rustles as it stands;
Within itself it thunders as it stands;
Within itself it roars as there it stands;
Within it there is much soft rain.
Around it four times did I circle
And toward the sea a branch I broke with all
    my force.
I took it and to you I brought it."
Therewith a part of the sickness
Did I pound into the earth and stake it down.

There was toward the sunrise
A white road made and finished.
Four stops made the youth and speedily did come
Where stood a white ocotillo.
Not slowly back to me he came and said:

"Within itself it rustles as it stands;
Within itself it thunders as it stands;
Within itself it roars as there it stands;
Within there is soft rain.
Around it four times did I circle
And toward the sunrise a branch I broke with all
    my force.
I took it and to you I brought it."
Therewith a part of the sickness
Did I pound into the ground and stake it down.

There was toward the north a red road made
    and finished.
Four stops made the youth and speedily did come
Where stood a red ocotillo.
Not slowly back to me he came and said:

"Within itself it rustles as it stands;
Within itself it thunders as it stands;
Within itself it roars as there it stands;
Within it there is much soft rain.
Four times around it did I circle
And toward the north a branch I broke with all
      my force.
I took it and to you I brought it."
Therewith a part of the sickness
Did I pound into the ground and stake it down.

Then forth came black tarantula magician.
In four places did he bite the earth and continue
      biting.
Some remaining shreds of sickness did he then
      fold up,
Did pound them into the earth and stake them
      down.

Then forth came the red wasp magicians.
In four places did they bite the earth and
      continue biting.
In four places did they make the earth into clay
      jars.
Into them did they pour some of the sickness,
Did pound them into the earth and stake them
      down.

From above descended mighty winged birds.
Their own wing feathers did they pull out
And therewith whipped and scattered some of
      the sickness.
All gone they thought it.

Then came forth the little sleeping people [ants].
Entering my house in ceaseless journeys,
The food [that caused my sickness] did they take
And yonder toward the north wind did they
    send it.

Then did the moisture that lies above begin to
    fall
And altogether did destroy the sickness.

Thus you also always think, all you my kinsmen.

PLEASURE AND PROFIT

IN ALL THE OLD DAYS, playing games took up fully half of an Indian's life. Dancing took up another large part, but was not counted as recreation; it was part of a religious service which helped to keep the world going. So were games in the very early days, when kicking a ball stuffed with seeds helped the seeds to sprout, and running races encouraged the sun on its course. But in most Indian tribes in the days before the Whites changed everything, games were the whole occupation for the leisure of man and woman, and they were the one real method of trade. Anyone writing a book on Indian economics might do worse than start with the subject of games; for all games included betting, whether they were athletic contests for the young men or games of chance for which the old people squatted on the sand throwing dice to the accompaniment of solemn song.

The Papagos have reduced gaming to a great intervillage system. Of course, neighbors dice together of an afternoon or bet on the speed of their barefoot sons and daughters over a mile of parched adobe race track. But this is only by way of preparation for the great yearly event when a whole group of villagers goes en masse to play with another group. Our intercollegiate football games with their national importance and their ardent local loyalties are the nearest parallel. The challenge is issued a year beforehand and the young men train like our own professionals. The favorite game is kickball, in which a wooden ball the size of a croquet ball is hurled along the ground with the bare foot. Men grow toenails to suit their profession, and old men with feet as brown and knobbed as tree roots sometimes have yellowed horns on their toes a quarter-inch thick. The course is thirty miles. A distant mountain is the goal, and the runners must steer their way around it through scrub and gravel and cactus, back to the village. Four or five men from each side kick the same ball, unless they fall from exhaustion, and horsemen follow to cheer them on. This is the game; or else it is relay racing, or dicing with carved and painted sticks, or hiding a bean in a pile of sand and guessing its whereabouts.

But there are preliminaries of high solemnity. The challenging visitors always sing for their hosts, and the hosts pay "because they have come so far

A Papago runner at the games

and have suffered on the way, and because they have entertained us with beautiful singing." This singing has been practiced for months, and costumes and a dance go with it. In fact, the entertainment is a rudimentary operetta. Some man dreams a whole series of songs about the wind or the clouds or about the white cranes that fly from the ocean. Then he gathers a score of boys and girls, who must be lithe of body and with long and glossy hair, and to them he teaches dance maneuvers which are like a quadrille or a European contradance.

Then he gathers all the old men skilled in the use of their hands, and under his direction they make the properties for the ballet: rainbows of painted buckskin stretched over flexible wands; white birds of raw cotton with painted wooden bills; mountains of buckskin with cotton clouds. The Desert People have almost no materials to work with. They contrive their effigies out of desert plants, buckskin, and the precious raw cotton, painting them with red and yellow clay and blue-black soot. But their entertainment is worth paying for with all the garnered food of the challenged village. Furthermore, it has the effect of every worthy effort in Papago life: it brings rain.

The songs which follow are sung while a group of boys and girls skip to and fro, combining and recombining, and carrying in their raised hands white birds and rainbows.

Dancers at the intervillage games

Crane birds!
Side by side in a row!

———

You go a little way and spread out.
Behind you, it is raining.

———

The mist I summon.
It comes: the earth is wet.
Then, as I walk, I sink deep in the earth.
I stand in the midst of the land.
I think it good.

———

In the night
The rain comes down.
Yonder at the edge of the earth
There is a sound like cracking,
There is a sound like falling.
Down yonder it goes on slowly rumbling,
It goes on shaking.

Sometimes the visitors sing songs extolling the names
of prominent men in the challenged village. As a rule,
no man lightly mentions another man's name, for fear
of using up its magic power; but to use it in this auspi-
cious connection is to bring the owner luck, and each
man sung for responds with a gift.

Is it your fame which comes forth, loud
     sounding?
Is it your fame which comes forth, loud
     sounding,
Juan Enos, your fame, far sounding?
It girds the enemy mountain
Like a bandoleer.

Over there came one.
Upon the flat land
There sounded stamping.
At Tecolote, Big Coyote,
Having killed an enemy,
Sang.
Over there came one.
Upon the flat land
There sounded stamping.

———————

Over there came one.
Upon the mountains
There sounded rattling.
At Wupatahi, Big Acacia,
Having killed an enemy,
Sang.
Over there came one.
Upon the mountains
There sounded rattling.

SONGS TO AID THE RUNNERS

Toward the west
Songs were sounding.
Excited I rushed forth.
I met the bitter wind
And tossed it up like a ball.

Toward the west
Songs were sounding.
Excited I rushed forth.
I met the sun
And tossed it up like a ball.

I come forth running,
I come forth running.
Bearing a cloud on my head,
I come forth running.

———

I speed my kickball.
Over the flat ground it runs.
Between the spreading branches
It settles down.

———

The hawk laid out the race track,
The hawk laid out the race track,
And on it the man won.

Wild the man came here,
Wild the man came here.
A hawk's heart he won.

SONGS OF TODAY

SOME PAPAGO CEREMONIES, although in our account of them we have used the present tense, are no longer practiced. Such are the war ceremonies, for the Apaches were subdued by the United States government, and no old man living has been to war. But all the other feasts are still held, some in one part of the reservation, some in another.

The rain house, the dome of brush without window or smoke hole, still stands in every principal village, though all the other houses are of adobe, in the Mexican manner. Within some rain houses the liquor is still fermented once a year, while the people sing outside. Within some the basket drums are scraped to sing up the corn or to drive away evil. Before some the deer flesh is still eaten to cleanse the town of sickness, though one Catholic hamlet has changed the ceremony to the killing of a steer before the church, with the blessing of the priest.

But songs are still being dreamed. Since the rigid poetic pattern of olden days has been relaxed, there is, perhaps, more humor and more variety in the songs of desert life, which the animal visitants teach. And to those animals that cause and cure sickness there have been added three white man's importations: the horse, the cow, and the devil. These teach their protégés entire series of songs no less vivid than those of the hawk and the coyote.

Even the dreaming and performance of operettas is not obsolete. One of the northern villages has an ancient Keeper of the Smoke who at one time was very ill. In his delirium he dreamed a series of songs to which the youths and maidens of his village have been dancing for two years. The subject of the series is a fitting close to a book of Papago songs.

The old man found himself in a city "far under the east" where the streets were like rocky canyons. There he saw the clown who dances at Papago ceremonies, wandering lost. The clown said he had been spirited to this strange city because someone had taken his photograph and transported it thither. Of course, the body of the clown then had to follow, even against his will. But, with the old man there, the clown felt strength to return.

The clown went, singing, back to the west, and the old man followed. "There wonderful things were seen." Among them was an ancient rain house, made of brush and hung with all the trappings of Papago ceremony. There were the masks of the harvest singers; there were the cotton "clouds"; there, too, were the woman's grinding slab, and the man's bow and arrow.

"Look at these things," said the clown. "Our people are ceasing to use them. It may be that this is right and that they should take over the white man's ways. But, before you decide, come here. Look once more at the old things. Be sure."